**HOBBES:
THE P**

HOBBES: A GUIDE FOR THE PERPLEXED

STEPHEN FINN

continuum

Continuum International Publishing Group
The Tower Building
11 York Road
London SE1 7NX
80 Maiden Lane
Suite 704
New York, NY 10038
www.continuumbooks.com

British Library Cataloging-in-Publication Data
A catalogue record for this book is available from the British Library.

ISBN-10: HB: 0-8264-8837-4; PB 0-8264-8838-2
ISBN-13: HB: 9780826488374; PB 9780826488381

Library of Congress Cataloguing-in-Publication Data
A catalog record for this book is available from the Library of Congress.

Typeset by Servis Filmsetting Ltd, Manchester
Printed and bound in Great Britain by
Athenaeum Press Ltd, Gateshead, Tyne and Wear

CONTENTS

CONTENTS

ACKNOWLEDGEMENTS

I would like to thank my colleague John Bean of the Seattle University English Department for his many insightful comments on my manuscript. Thanks also to David Blancha, my research assistant and philosophy major at Seattle University, for his help in making the manuscript more accessible to students and to a general readership. I would also like to thank Hywel Evans for inviting me to contribute to the *Guides for the Perplexed* series. I am also grateful to Sarah Douglas, the editor of this volume, for her patience and her assistance. Finally, thanks to my wife Joan for her encouragement and support.

For my son, Seamus

A NOTE TO READERS

This book is a guide not only to understanding the thought of Thomas Hobbes, but also to the philosophical activities of *interpretation* and *enquiry*. There are many excellent books that introduce Hobbes's philosophy to a general audience, so one might wonder why another book is needed. This book is unique, I believe, insofar as it encourages readers not only to develop their own *interpretation* of Hobbes, but also to engage in a philosophical *enquiry* into the ideas that Hobbes addresses. In this note, I would like to offer a few preliminary comments about how to use this book.

I suspect that you are reading this book on Hobbes to learn about his ideas. You should be aware, however, that scholars frequently disagree about what Hobbes's ideas really are. Thus, when you read an introductory text on Hobbes, including this one, you will often read a specific interpretation of Hobbes that may differ from other interpretations of Hobbes. On even some of the most basic ideas in Hobbes's philosophy, there is scholarly disagreement. In the end, then, you must determine for yourself whether a specific interpretation is accurate. To make this determination, you must read Hobbes's texts on your own and not simply rely on a guide to tell you what he said. To begin your interpretation of Hobbes, the present guide should serve you well. The second section of each chapter contains numerous passages from Hobbes's works that provide enough material for your own interpretation. For best results, however, I recommend that you acquire Hobbes's original texts, either through purchase or library loan, and refer to them when you wish to understand the context of a specific textual passage quoted in this book. Most of the Hobbes quotations used in this book are taken from one of his three main political works (*Elements of Law*, *De Cive* and

Leviathan) or from his work on natural philosophy (*De Corpore*). I use the following abbreviations.

Ci *De Cive* in B. Gert (ed.), *Thomas Hobbes: Man and Citizen*. Indianapolis: Hackett Publishing, 1991.
Co *De Corpore* in W. Molesworth (ed.), *The English Works of Thomas Hobbes of Malmesbury*. London: John Bohn, Vol. 1, 1841.
El *Elements of Law Natural and Politic*, F. Toennies (ed.). London: Frank Cass & Co., 1969.
L *Leviathan*, C.B. Macpherson (ed.). London: Penguin Classics, 1985.

All parenthetical references are to chapter and page number, with the exception of those from the *Elements of Law*, which are to part, chapter and section number. Quotations from the *Elements of Law* are taken from an out-of-print version edited by Ferdinand Toennies. There is, however, an affordable and readily available paperback edition: *Elements of Law Natural and Politic*, J.C.A. Gaskin (ed.). Oxford: Oxford University Press, 1994. When I refer to the *Elements of Law*, I use part, chapter and section numbers, e.g., *El* 1.1.2 refers to *Elements of Law*, Part I, Chapter 1, Section 2. The Toennies edition and the Gaskin edition have the same chapter numbers in Part I. However, in Part II, the Toennies edition starts again at Chapter 1, while the Gaskin edition starts at Chapter 20, where Part I left off. If you are using the Gaskin edition, you should still be able to follow along. The editions of both *Leviathan* and *De Cive* listed above are readily available in paperback. Unfortunately, *De Corpore* is an out-of-print and rare book. If you wish to refer to *De Corpore*, you may have to obtain it through an inter-library loan. A small number of selected chapters of *De Corpore* are included as an appendix to the *Elements of Law* edited by Gaskin. In cases where I refer to or use passages from other texts of Hobbes, or other texts in general, I have referenced them in endnotes.

It should also be noted that I have modernized spelling and modified punctuation of Hobbes's original texts in many places to make the texts easier to read.

PREFACE: INTERPRETATION AND ENQUIRY

I am occasionally asked by friends and family what it is that philosophers really do when they are not teaching. From my personal experience, there seems to be a common misperception that we spend our days thinking about traditional philosophical questions: What is the purpose of life? Is there a God? Do we have a soul? What is truth? Why should one be moral? In actuality, philosophy professors devote much of their time to reading the works of past philosophers. Reading philosophy, as you may already know, is no easy task. The abstract nature of its concepts, the indeterminateness of its questions and the seemingly impenetrable language of its writers often combine to make reading philosophy mentally challenging. To complicate matters even further, a philosophical text is often subject to a variety of incompatible interpretations. Two different people reading the same text might disagree about 'what it means'. One of the main activities of contemporary philosophers is to *interpret* texts in order to reveal and understand their meaning. Scholars in today's academic world of philosophy usually make their careers by becoming specialists of a particular philosophical figure or period. Interestingly, even specialists in the same area will disagree over what a particular philosophical text means. In part, this book is a guide to the philosophical activity of *interpretation*. More specifically, it is concerned with interpreting the thought of Thomas Hobbes, a seventeenth-century Englishman who is often considered to be one of the most important philosophers in history. In this book, you will be challenged to participate in the activity of interpretation and to decide for yourself which of the many interpretations of Hobbes's philosophy is the most reasonable.

Of course, philosophers would not be philosophers if they did not also partake in philosophical *enquiry*, i.e., delve into the philosophical issues themselves and attempt to uncover the truth, if there is such a thing. We read philosophical texts of the past not simply to understand the ideas of important philosophers, but also to 'do philosophy'. In other words, we want not only to be informed about previous answers to philosophical questions, but to make our own *enquiry* into the issues. We need to enquire into the rationality of various philosophical beliefs. We need to question which position on a given issue is the most reasonable. Even if there are no definitive answers to a number of philosophical questions, this does not mean the task is hopeless. Instead, we should try hard to find the best answers to philosophical questions, even if we cannot be sure the best ones are the right ones. In this book, you will be encouraged not only to interpret the thought of Hobbes, but also to use his ideas as a starting point for your own enquiry into pressing philosophical issues.

This book is divided thematically in that each of the following chapters, with the exception of Chapters 1 and 7, focuses on one of the five major branches of Hobbes's philosophy. It should be noted that the branches of philosophy, as treated in this book, are based upon today's view of philosophy and its main divisions. For Hobbes, as we shall see in the next chapter, there are only three branches of philosophy. In Chapter 1, I provide an overview of Hobbes's philosophy and a brief introduction to the tools of interpretation and enquiry. In Chapters 2 through to 6, I present a summary of Hobbes's philosophical ideas in the following areas of philosophy: epistemology, metaphysics, moral philosophy, political philosophy and the philosophy of religion. Chapter 7 concludes by revisiting some of the interpretative issues raised in the book and raising one final interpretative question. If you are unfamiliar with any of these terms, they will be defined at the start of the appropriate chapter. In addition to a summary of Hobbes's ideas, each chapter also contains an Interpretation section and an Enquiry section. In the Interpretation sections I will usually present two conflicting interpretations of Hobbes and then encourage you to form your own view based upon a close reading of specific passages from his texts. The Enquiry sections take the next step beyond interpretation. They raise the question of whether Hobbes was right by challenging you to consider competing philosophical positions. It will be up to you to determine for yourself which of the competing positions is philosophically the strongest. While I may, in some cases, present some of the strengths and weaknesses of particular positions, I will not press any of them. It is your job to shape your own philosophy by applying your own natural ability to reason.

Although this book is part of the 'Guides for the Perplexed' series, you should be aware that the job of a philosophical guide is not always to guide you *out* of perplexity. Instead, as the author of this philosophical guide, I believe it is my responsibility to lead you into a state of perplexity and to force you to respond. Part of the work of doing philosophy, as I see it, is to find your own way out of confusing and perplexing issues. To help you in this regard, I have included a number of 'perplexing problems' throughout the book. The perplexing problems will frequently ask you to take Hobbes's place and to explain apparent inconsistencies or problems in his texts. Taking on the role of Hobbes will help you enter into the practice of philosophy.

CHAPTER 1

INTRODUCTION TO HOBBES AND THE BASICS OF INTERPRETATION AND ENQUIRY

Imagine that you are in a foreign city without any maps, guidebooks or other sources of information. In such a case, you may decide that the best way to come to know the city is by wandering through the streets, visiting one neighbourhood at a time. But where should you start? In which direction should you walk? If it is a large city with complicated street patterns, it may take a long time for you to understand the spatial relationships of the city's neighbourhoods. You may miss some of its important points of interest. Of course, over time, you may come to know the city very well. If at the start, however, you were given a map with a layout of the city and with marked points of interest, you would more quickly be able to take advantage of your stay. Reading a philosopher for the first time is like entering a new city without a map. It seems reasonable to begin by reading a text by the philosopher, but which one should you start with? Which text should you read after that? To help you travel in Hobbes's world, I will first provide a map, or overview, of his philosophical ideas. By knowing a little about his life, his place in the history of philosophy, the main ideas of his philosophical system and the relevance of his philosophy today, you will find it easier to read his philosophical texts and enter his philosophical world. In the first section of this chapter, I present an overview of Hobbes's life and his philosophy. As we shall see, Hobbes lived during a time of great political unrest. His primary philosophical goal, at least in his political philosophy, was to provide a solution to the problem of civil war. Hobbes did not only practise political philosophy, but he also pursued his interests in ethical, religious and historical topics, as the variety of his works attests. In the second section of this chapter, I introduce some tools that will help you interpret Hobbes on

your own. As you will see, there are a variety of approaches to interpreting philosophy: there is no standard way of doing it. In the
third section, I present some basic ideas concerning philosophical
enquiry. Most contemporary philosophers would probably agree
that philosophical enquiry should be guided by reason and that the
best answers in philosophy are the most rational.

I. SUMMARY: HOBBES'S LIFE AND PHILOSOPHY

The Life and Works of Thomas Hobbes

Hobbes was born prematurely on 5 April 1588 in an English village
called Westport in Somerset. He jokingly blamed his mother's fear
of the impending invasion of the Spanish Armada for his early
arrival. Although the historical facts do not corroborate this explanation (the Armada set sail a month after his birth), there may be
some truth to it, since Hobbes's mother may have been frightened
simply by rumours of an invasion. Hobbes's father, Thomas senior,
was a minister of the Church of England who was fond of drinking
and gambling. Thomas senior left his family behind, never to be seen
again, when Hobbes was 16. In 1608, after finishing his formal education, Hobbes was hired by the aristocrat William Cavendish to
tutor his son, also named William Cavendish. The connection with
this family provided Hobbes with ample opportunities to meet
important intellectuals all over Europe. On two occasions, for
example, Hobbes accompanied a Cavendish on a European trip
where he would have dealings with, among others, the scientist
Galileo, the mathematician Marin Mersenne and the astronomer
Pierre Gassendi.

Hobbes did not publish any philosophical or scientific works until
later in his life. In 1628, when Hobbes was 40 years old, he published
the first work of his literary career. This was a translation of
Thucydides' *History of the Peloponnesian Wars*. Hobbes probably
started to translate Thucydides' work in the 1620s, while conflict
between Charles I and parliament escalated. In 1626, Charles I
requested from parliament funds to pursue war against Spain and
France. Parliament denied Charles's request and he responded with
a Forced Loan, by which he demanded that individual subjects loan
him money. The unpopularity of this policy increased political ten-
sions in England. The Forced Loan led directly to the Five Knights

Case, which itself magnified the problems. The case started with the imprisonment of knights for refusing to pay the loan. The knights filed a Habeas Corpus suit and demanded that the king reveal the reason for their imprisonment. The king's attorney asserted that the knights were imprisoned *per special mandatum domini reges* (by special command of the king). This case raised important political questions about the limits of the king's right to rule. Are the king's actions limited by the law? If so, does the king have the right to act outside the law when circumstances require it? Answers to such questions exposed serious ideological differences between king and parliament. Given this historical context, it is likely that Hobbes considered the publication of his translation to be a political act. In his autobiography, Hobbes claimed that Thucydides' *History* teaches the important lesson that democracy is 'inadequate' and that the wisdom of one person is much greater than the wisdom of many. Over the next two decades, Hobbes developed his own political philosophy, which was presented in three versions: the *Elements of Law* (1640), *De Cive* (1641) and *Leviathan* (1651). While there are important differences among these works, the basic argument remains the same: Hobbes argues for the superiority of an absolutist form of government. In his view, peace requires a strong sovereign power that has the final say on all matters political, ethical and religious. Questioning the king's authority, in Hobbes's opinion, ultimately leads to division in the commonwealth and, eventually, to civil war. So it is better to live with the 'inconveniences' of a powerful leader than to be in a state of war.

Shortly after the publication of the *Elements of Law*, long-time supporters of the king were executed by parliament. Hobbes, out of fear for his own life, decided to flee to France, where he would stay for more than a decade. During this period of his life, Hobbes ventured into other areas of philosophy. He wrote numerous polemical works that attacked many philosophical ideas of his contemporaries. In 1641, for example, Hobbes published objections to Descartes' *Meditations on First Philosophy*. Descartes, a contemporary of Hobbes, argued that reality was composed of two kinds of substances: spiritual and material. In response, Hobbes argued that reality consisted only of material bodies. A year later, Hobbes wrote a criticism of Thomas White's *De Mundo*, which included many philosophical and scientific ideas that would eventually appear in his treatise on natural science. Shortly thereafter, Hobbes composed a series of letters in response to Bishop Bramhall, a Catholic theologian who was critical of Hobbes's view of the human will. Hobbes returned to England in 1651, the year in which *Leviathan* was published. In *Leviathan*, which is considered his masterpiece, Hobbes not only expands upon the political arguments found in the *Elements of Law* and *De Cive*, but also offers a more developed theological argument. As in the earlier works, Hobbes argues in the first two parts of *Leviathan* for the necessity of an absolute sovereign. The political arguments of *Leviathan* rely upon the power of natural reason to reach their conclusions. In Parts III and IV, however, Hobbes uses extended biblical interpretation to support his political arguments. Although Hobbes had done something similar in the other political works, the theological argument of *Leviathan* is more thorough, forceful and rhetorical in its use of biblical exegesis.

After the publication of *Leviathan*, Hobbes focused on the study of mathematics and natural science. In 1655, Hobbes published *De Corpore*, which develops his views on philosophical methodology, geometry and physics. During this period of his life, many eminent mathematicians and scientists ridiculed Hobbes's scientific ideas, especially his ideas on geometry. Hobbes defended himself by writing a number of works in these areas. During this later period of his life, Hobbes not only continued his work in natural philosophy, but also revisited political issues, this time through an historical perspective. In 1668, Hobbes completed *Behemoth: Or the Long Parliament*, which contains his account of the English Civil War. In this work, Hobbes points out that the political conflicts of his lifetime were primarily the result of the seditious opinions of 'seducers and demagogues' trying to usurp the king's power. In *A Dialogue between a Philosopher and a Student of the Common Laws of England,* Hobbes argued against the view of lawyer Edward Coke that the law is above the king. Consistent with the opinions expressed in his political works, Hobbes once again argued that the king should have been allowed to act outside the scope of the law for the benefit of the commonwealth. In his final years, Hobbes finished where he had started, in a sense, by returning to translation. His last works were translations of Homer's *Iliad* and *Odyssey*. After becoming seriously ill in 1679, Hobbes suffered a stroke in late November and died a week later.

The Branches of Hobbes's Philosophy

In *De Cive*, Hobbes divides philosophy into three branches, each of which studies a different kind of 'body': natural, human and political (*Ci* Preface: 102–3). *Natural philosophy*, Hobbes says, studies the fundamental properties of bodies in the natural world. This branch of philosophy includes physics, which investigates, for example, the motions of the stars and planets, the effects of gravity or the growth of plants and trees. In Hobbes's time, scientists such as Galileo were called 'natural philosophers' because they studied the natural world. Since natural philosophy uses both mathematics and geometry, it includes these sciences as well. Hobbes's natural philosophy is guided by the fundamental belief in *mechanistic materialism*, which, as the name suggests, claims that the universe is like a *machine* (i.e. a mechanism) and is composed only of *material* bodies. According to Hobbes, there are no spirits or souls, if these refer to incorporeal (non-physical) entities. Instead, the universe is comprised only of bodies that operate according to strict scientific laws of cause and effect. Every event, in other words, is caused by some other temporally prior event. The goal of natural philosophy is to understand the causes of physical motions by reducing all events and things to their fundamental motions. If we want to understand how a watch works, for example, we should take it apart and see how the parts interact.

The second branch of Hobbes's philosophy is *moral philosophy*, which specifically studies human bodies. Of course, humans are physical bodies in the world. If a person falls out of a tree, for example, he or she will be pulled to the ground by the force of gravity, just like any other natural body. In other words, human beings can be the subject matter of both natural philosophy and moral philosophy. Unfortunately, Hobbes does not draw the line clearly between natural philosophy and moral philosophy when it comes to understanding human bodies. This lack of clarity is revealed in *Leviathan*, for example, where Hobbes divides philosophy into only two branches: natural philosophy and political philosophy. In this case, 'ethics' (which is another term for moral philosophy) is a subdivision of natural philosophy (*L* 9.149). Yet as we have seen in *De Cive*, Hobbes claims there are three branches of philosophy. This confusion is indicative of a larger interpretative problem that will be discussed in the concluding chapter of this book. For now, however, we must recognize that human bodies can be studied from different perspectives, depending upon whether we are looking at them simply as natural objects or as beings with emotions, feelings and other psychological qualities. Moral philosophy, for Hobbes, is not concerned with human beings insofar as they are like inert bodies; instead, it studies such aspects of our nature as our actions, emotions and states of mind. However, in keeping with his view of nature, Hobbes's description of these human properties or events is *mechanistic*. In other words, we are similar to machines, but machines with mental states and emotions. As Hobbes sees it, physical objects and events in the natural world start a series of internal 'motions' that ultimately cause not only our thoughts, but also our behaviour. So, for example, if a barking dog approaches me, I will become fearful, which will lead me to protect myself in some manner. The dog, in other words, caused fear in my mind, which, in turn, caused me to take action. Most human actions, if not all of them, Hobbes says, are motivated by the desire to achieve the 'good'. As Hobbes sees it, the individual desires of each person ultimately determine what is good or bad. For example, if I desire a piece of cake, the cake is 'good' to me. If another person wishes to avoid eating cake, then the cake is 'bad'. What is good or bad is relative to each individual; there is no standard of goodness or badness that applies to all individuals. To put this another way, Hobbes adheres to what is called a *subjective notion of the good*.

The third branch of Hobbes's philosophy, *political philosophy*, deals with political bodies. In this branch of philosophy, Hobbes considers, among other things, the origin, maintenance and justification of political institutions. Hobbes's primary goal in his political philosophy is to establish a 'science of politics'. According to Hobbes, the serious political problems of his time resulted from disagreements over who has the ultimate authority in political and religious affairs. If a method to prove political truths could be found, Hobbes believed, then such disagreements could be averted and peace firmly secured. Hobbes found a methodological model for his political science in geometry. In the science of geometry, practitioners prove their conclusions on the basis of self-evident or commonly accepted principles. Hobbes, mimicking the method of geometry, attempts to ground his political argument on the 'obvious truth' of human behaviour (i.e. that humans are ultimately motivated to achieve their own good). If this truth is recognized, Hobbes believes, then conclusions may be drawn with which no rational person could disagree. The main conclusion of Hobbes's political philosophy is that peace in a commonwealth requires an *absolute sovereign power* that has the final say on all political and religious matters. In the process of making his political argument, Hobbes employs the concept of the 'state of nature', which is a hypothetical state with no laws, legal enforcement or other aspects of organized society. In such a state, Hobbes argues, humans would be constantly at war with each other because individuals would seek their own good and not recognize any universal standards of behaviour. An absolute sovereign would prevent conflict by creating laws and a system to enforce those laws. If people begin to disobey the sovereign, they will ultimately return to a state of nature,which is beneficial to no one.

Matter in Motion

The various branches of philosophy, as Hobbes sees it, are all sciences of motion. In keeping with his mechanistic materialism, reality is ultimately comprised of 'matter in motion'. If you want to understand a given thing or event, you must understand the 'motions' that brought it into being. Hobbes believes, for example, that geometry is a science of motion because it is concerned with the construction of figures through the motion of points: 'a line is made by the motion of a point, superficies by the motion of a line, and one motion by another motion' (*Co* 6.70). Geometric figures, in other words, are constructed by the movement of a point through space. Physics also is a science of motion because it is an 'enquiry of such effects as are made by the motion of the parts of any body' (*Co* 6.72). Moral philosophy, Hobbes says, studies the 'motions of the mind, namely, appetite, aversion, love, benevolence, hope, fear, anger, emulation, envy, &c.; what causes they have and of what they be causes' (*Co* 6.72). Given the fact that such emotions are ultimately reducible to physical motions in the human body, it makes sense that moral philosophy is a science of motion. Through knowledge of the motions of the mind, one discovers the motions by which a commonwealth is created. The 'principles of politics', Hobbes says, 'consist in the knowledge of the motions of the mind' (*Co* 6.74).

Hobbes and the History of Philosophy

Hobbes practised philosophy in what is now called the *modern period* of philosophy. In many philosophy textbooks, Hobbes's contemporary, René Descartes, is often referred to as the 'father of modern philosophy'. If Hobbes were alive today, he would probably try to lay claim to that title himself. In any event, modern philosophers were challenging the ideas of the *medieval period* of philosophy. While there are numerous differences between these two periods, one of the most important is the contrast between their respective philosophical goals. During the Middle Ages, Christian philosophers (or, perhaps more appropriately, theologians) wanted to deepen their understanding of God and Christian faith. To do so, medieval philosophers employed reason to interpret and to make sense of certain texts, especially the Bible and the philosophical works of Aristotle. It is interesting that Aristotle, who lived before the time of Jesus in the *ancient period* of philosophy, was recognized as 'the philosopher' – the one classical philosopher who expounded the truth about nature, human life and ultimate reality. Accepting the authority of both the Bible and Aristotle, medieval philosophers tried to synthesize the philosophical ideas of this ancient Greek philosopher with their Christian beliefs. It is often claimed that philosophy was simply the 'handmaiden to theology' in the medieval period. By contrast, modern philosophers, such as Descartes and Hobbes, believed that human reason is sufficient for acquiring philosophical knowledge; in other words, one does not need to rely upon the authority of others to find the truth. When you read Hobbes's original texts, you may find him to be very critical of the 'Schools', meaning the scholastic education that relied on authoritative texts. Modern philosophers also stressed the importance of philosophical method for acquiring truth. With a correct method in place, modern philosophers believed, any rational person could discover the truth for him- or herself.

The Contemporary Relevance of Hobbes

Why is Hobbes philosophically relevant today? In my opinion, there are three important reasons why you should study Hobbes's philosophy. First, Hobbes stands in a long tradition of philosophers who attempted to answer, in a systematic way, the most perplexing questions of human life. Even if all or most of Hobbes's philosophical answers are inadequate, the process of examining and evaluating his arguments is a fruitful process for our own philosophical investigations. What issues did Hobbes find important? How did he defend his philosophical positions? What were his goals for philosophy? Where did he go wrong? In what ways was he right? Answering such questions is a good way to start our own philosophical enquiry. Second, Hobbes raises an important philosophical question that still demands an answer today: What is the best form of government in states where individuals have divergent religious, moral and political views? Although Hobbes was primarily concerned with finding a way to avoid civil war, international war is a constant in our world. Even if we are not convinced by Hobbes's political solution, the question of how to avoid war and conflict is an important question to raise. Third, Hobbes's view of human nature, i.e., that humans are basically selfish, is a dominant idea in today's world that influences our actions. When I ask my students what the world would be like if the government were dissolved, the police force disbanded, and all structures in society dismantled, they frequently provide a Hobbesian answer, i.e., that there would be a state of anarchy. It seems to me that many people (especially my students) implicitly accept Hobbes's view that humans are basically selfish and need to be restrained by force into lawful obedience. By reading Hobbes, we may bring this implicit acceptance of Hobbes's view to light and critically evaluate it.

II. INTERPRETATION: THE BASICS OF PHILOSOPHICAL INTERPRETATION

Many present-day philosophers spend a great deal of time on the *interpretation* of *primary* philosophical texts. A primary philosophical text is an original work of a particular philosopher that presents his or her own ideas. A secondary text, on the other hand, is one that explores, clarifies, summarizes or elaborates upon the ideas of a primary text. So, for example, Hobbes's *Leviathan* is a primary text; the book you are reading right now is a secondary text. Primary texts, like paintings, poems or songs, may often be interpreted in a variety of ways. Two different individuals reading a passage from Hobbes's *Leviathan*, for example, may disagree over its 'meaning'. This book is intended, in part, to be a guide to help you *interpret* Hobbes's primary texts on your own. In the *Interpretation* section of each remaining chapter, we look at specific passages from Hobbes's texts that may be interpreted in different ways. After a close study of these passages, you will be encouraged to decide for yourself which interpretation, if any, is the best. Before we get to that point, however, some introductory comments about interpretation ought to be presented.

Interpretation and its Goals

What is the main goal of interpreting a primary philosophical text? As you may expect, philosophers themselves answer this question differently. Some philosophers, for example, claim that the goal of interpretation is to understand and reveal the text's 'meaning', which is identified with the author's intended thoughts. In writing *Leviathan*, for example, Hobbes obviously intended to express his own ideas about certain topics. One could reasonably argue, therefore, that the job of interpreting *Leviathan* is to correctly identify and make known *Hobbes's* ideas. However, one could also plausibly argue that a text, once it has been written and committed to paper, has a philosophical meaning of its own. In this case, one should not ask what Hobbes intended to say, but what the text itself says. Here, an interpreter would probably be more interested in examining the arguments of the text to see if they are good arguments. In addition, an interpreter may wish to develop and improve upon the arguments themselves, regardless of what Hobbes would have intended. The contrast between these different goals might seem a little strange at first, but when you consider other forms of human expression, especially those in the realm of art, it begins to make more sense. Is the 'meaning' of your favourite song, for example, the same as what the songwriter intended to express? Or, do you find your own meaning in the song? Of course, the goals of artists should not simply be identified with those of philosophers; nevertheless, philosophers and artists could be viewed as the producers of works that have their own life and meaning. Although people may disagree about whether the meaning of a text lies in the author's intentions or in the text itself, I would like to stress that the two goals of interpretation just stated are not mutually exclusive. An interpreter of Hobbes, for example, may wish to find out both what Hobbes intended and what the text itself says. In my opinion, both of these tasks would be included in a philosopher's job description.

Dealing with Inconsistencies

One of the main tasks for philosophical interpreters, including interpreters of Hobbes, is to resolve inconsistencies in the primary texts.

Philosophers, especially those who have a long literary career, may make claims that are inconsistent, or seemingly inconsistent, with other claims they have made. As an example, let's take the following two statements of Hobbes:

(A) 'For every man is desirous of what is good for him and shuns what is evil, but chiefly the chiefest of natural evils, which is death' (*Ci* 1.115).

(B) A 'son would rather die than live infamous and hated of all the world' (*Ci* 6.183).

In (A), Hobbes apparently claims that *all* people naturally desire to avoid death. In (B), however, Hobbes suggests that a person may actually desire death. Is there an inconsistency here? If you believe there is no inconsistency, then you need to explain how the *apparently* inconsistent claims are consistent. On the other hand, if you believe the claims are not consistent, then you should try to resolve the inconsistency by offering a reasonable explanation for it. There are a variety of ways to deal with inconsistent statements of a philosopher.

(1) *The Apparent Inconsistency Approach*: Interpreters may explain apparent inconsistencies by showing that the given inconsistency is precisely that, i.e., *apparent*. One could carefully examine the terms of the seemingly inconsistent statements and show that there really is no inconsistency. So, for example, in (A) Hobbes does not explicitly say that all people always try to avoid death; he only says that people do not desire death. In addition, Hobbes does not claim in (B) that a son desires death; rather, he says that a son would choose death over another option. To choose, however, is not the same as to desire. Thus, the two claims are not inconsistent. Whether this resolution stands up to further scrutiny however, I leave for you to decide.

(2) *The Carelessness Approach*: Interpreters could explain inconsistencies by appealing to the carelessness of the philosopher. Simply put, philosophers make unintended mistakes when they write; upon being made aware of these mistakes, philosophers would probably adjust the statements to make them consistent. Of course, interpreters cannot point out inconsistencies to the dead, so they must imagine how a philosopher might have

responded to certain inconsistencies. Usually, interpreters use other statements of the philosopher to determine the author's real position on the matter. So, for example, interpreters could claim that Hobbes was careless when he said that 'every man' tries to avoid death. He probably meant to say 'almost every man'. Does this seem to be an adequate way to resolve the inconsistency?

(3) *The Maturation of Thought Approach*: Philosophers, like anyone, are human beings whose opinions change over time. When trying to resolve inconsistent statements made by the same philosopher, an interpreter should consider when the passages were written. If the statements were written 20 years apart, then perhaps the philosopher changed his or her mind. In our example, however, this is probably not a reasonable explanation since the two statements are taken from the same work. Yet, when you find other kinds of inconsistencies spread over many of Hobbes's works, perhaps this will seem like a reasonable approach to take.

(4) *The Esoteric Approach*: Some interpreters believe inconsistencies reveal a 'hidden' meaning that could not be explicitly stated. Afraid to express certain ideas because of dangerous political or social situations, philosophers may try to get their message across covertly. In this case, the real intention is not explicitly expressed, but lies beneath the surface. Inconsistencies in texts may therefore arise when a philosopher is explicitly stating one thing, but implying the opposite. As we shall see in Chapter 6, one could claim that Hobbes was an atheist despite his explicit claims to the contrary. On the one hand, Hobbes explicitly states that he is a Christian. On the other hand, many of his statements apparently undermine religious belief. It is difficult to see how the inconsistency found in (A) and (B) can be resolved by this approach. Nevertheless, when we examine other inconsistencies in Hobbes's thought, the power of political and social forces should not be completely disregarded since there are cases where authors of philosophical and scientific texts were obviously influenced by fear of punishment. In Hobbes's lifetime, Galileo, fearing reprisals from the Inquisition, used a fictional character in one of his works to defend covertly the theory of a heliocentric universe. Ultimately, the plan did not work as he was found guilty of heresy and placed under house arrest.

(5) *The Genuine Inconsistency Approach*: Interpreters, when unable

to resolve an inconsistency in any of the above ways, may simply give up. In this case, one does not really resolve the inconsistency so much as recognize that the philosopher's 'real' position is not attainable. So, for example, interpreters might claim that there is no way to resolve satisfactorily (A) and (B). What do you think about this approach?

As you read Hobbes, then, you should decide for yourself what kind of interpretative approach, if any, you favour. It is not necessary for you to choose just one. Instead, you may adapt your approach to suit the specific situation. Nevertheless, reading and interpreting philosophical works *requires* you to make such decisions.

III. ENQUIRY: THE BASICS OF PHILOSOPHICAL ENQUIRY

While present-day philosophers often adopt the role of interpreters, they also search for their own answers to philosophical questions: Is there a God? What is the nature of justice? Do humans have free will? Is the mind separate from the body? Does the soul exist? What is personal identity? Although it may be difficult, or even impossible, to answer such questions definitively, we should not be dissuaded from trying to find the most reasonable answers. We may never prove, for example, whether God exists or not. Nevertheless, should we not seek the *most reasonable* answer? Part of the goal of philosophical enquiry, then, is to find the most reasonable answers to the meaningful questions of life. In the *Enquiry* section of each remaining chapter, you will be encouraged to participate in the activity of philosophical enquiry. We will use Hobbes's philosophical positions as our starting point for this activity; rather than try to determine what Hobbes said, we will try to determine whether he was right. To do so, alternative positions on a given topic will be presented. It will then be your job to decide which position, if any, is philosophically stronger. Before we can do this, however, introductory comments on the activity of philosophical enquiry must be presented.

Conceptual Clarity

When one tries to answer a specific philosophical question, it is often necessary to define one's terms and to clarify the concepts involved. This is required because philosophical enquiry often deals with highly abstract concepts such as God, free will, the soul or justice. If we want to question whether God exists, then, it is reasonable for us first to define 'God'. Does 'God' refer to a personal being that cares for humans? Or does 'God' refer to an impersonal force that guides the cosmos without any concern for human life? Does 'God' refer to a male, female or a non-gendered being? As another example, let's assume that we want to argue that capitalism is an unjust economic system. For our argument to succeed, we must clarify the concept of injustice. What does it mean to say that something is unjust? Once we answer this question, we may then proceed to support our conclusion that capitalism is unjust. As you will see, clarifying concepts and defining one's terms is an important part of philosophical enquiry.

Philosophical Argumentation

Philosophers are expected not only to provide answers to philosophical questions, but also to defend their answers through argumentation. A philosopher who believes the death penalty is morally acceptable, for example, should provide an *argument* that tries to establish the reasonableness or superiority of this position. In philosophy, an argument is a statement or series of statements (referred to as the 'premises') that purport to support another statement (referred to as the 'conclusion'). For example, one could make the following argument in favour of the death penalty:

> *Premise 1:* The death penalty saves lives because it deters potential murderers from murdering people.
> *Premise 2:* If the death penalty saves lives, then it is morally acceptable.
> *Conclusion:* The death penalty is morally acceptable.

The premises are intended to work together to provide rational support for the conclusion that the death penalty is morally acceptable. The purpose of the argument, in other words, is to show that the conclusion is true and that any rational person should accept it.

An important part of philosophical enquiry is the *evaluation* of arguments. Although the author of the death penalty argument above intends it to be a good one, we must evaluate it and determine whether it is genuinely good. To evaluate an argument properly, we must ask two questions: (1) Do the premises actually support the conclusion and (2) Are the premises true? To ascertain whether the premises support the conclusion, *assume* that the premises are true and then ask whether the conclusion *follows* from the premises. When you do this, you are simply checking the *logic* of the argument. So, for example, referring to the death penalty argument, *if* the *first* two premises *were* true, then the conclusion does seem to follow. Logically, then, the death penalty argument seems to work. This, however, is not enough for us to say that it is a *good* argument. A good argument must also have true premises. To see this, consider the following argument:

> *Premise 1*: All US politicians are space aliens.
> *Premise 2*: Santa Claus is a US politician.
> *Conclusion*: Santa Claus is a space alien.

Although the premises logically support the conclusion, this does not mean that you should accept the conclusion that Santa Claus is a space alien. The conclusion of an argument should be accepted as true only if it meets both criteria, namely, that the premises support it and the premises are true. It should be noted that most philosophers do not lay out their arguments in a neat form, with premises and conclusions clearly marked. Instead, philosophers tend to elaborate on premises, discuss related ideas, make smaller arguments that play a role in a larger argument, provide evidence and/or go off on tangents. Even when one argument is enclosed within a short amount of textual space, it is still sometimes difficult to identify the steps of the argument.

How does one decide whether the premises of a philosophical argument are true? The answer to this question depends upon the kind of claim made in a given premise. The premises of a philosophical argument come in a variety of forms. First, some premises are empirical statements that may be directly confirmed or denied by appealing to the facts of the matter. So, for example, the number of prisoners convicted of murder in the New York State courts in 2005 is a readily available fact. Second, some premises are inferences derived from established facts. For instance, 'men have more political power than women' may be inferred from the fact that men hold more political offices than women. Third, a premise may contain a fundamental principle that cannot be confirmed or denied by appealing to facts. 'Every human being has a right to life' or 'a practice that saves lives is morally acceptable' are examples of such fundamental principles. With these distinctions in place, you are in a better position to determine whether the premises of an argument are true. Let us return to the death penalty argument mentioned above. The first premise claims that the death penalty saves lives because it deters potential murderers from murdering people. To decide whether this is true, one must recognize that this is not a statement of empirical fact. One cannot simply ask a 'potential murderer' whether the death penalty deterred him or her from committing a murder. Rather, one must try to confirm or refute it by inference from facts. For example, let us assume for the sake of argument that fewer murders occur in states *without* the death penalty. If this is true, then one might plausibly infer that the death penalty does not deter potential murderers since more murders occur even with the death penalty in place. Of course, one must use reason to determine whether such an inference is genuinely reasonable. For example, one might question whether the similarities between the two states are relevant to this issue. Are the two states demographically similar? Does one state have more cities, where murders are more likely to occur, than the other state? Are there other considerations that would influence this issue? Such questions need to be addressed before we can judge the truth or falsity of the first premise. The second premise of the death penalty argument says that the death penalty is a morally justified practice if it saves lives. To decide whether this is true, you cannot refer to an empirical fact nor can you draw such an inference from an empirical fact. What is or is not 'moral' is determined by a philosophical, not an empirical, enquiry. Does saving lives make the death penalty moral? Or does the sanctity of human life make the death penalty immoral no matter what? These kinds of questions you must ultimately answer for yourself. However, a number of philosophers, including Hobbes, have already tried to provide some reasonable answers. A good place to start your own philosophical enquiry, then, is by reading works of philosophers.

CONCLUSION

This summary of Hobbes's philosophy has been provided as a map to his philosophical thinking. It is my hope that by starting with a general picture of his philosophy, you will be better able to understand specific details when you encounter them. In this chapter, we have found that Hobbes lived a long life dedicated to the pursuit of philosophical knowledge. For Hobbes, philosophy attempts to understand a variety of bodies: natural, human and political. As such, for Hobbes, there are three branches of philosophy: natural philosophy, moral philosophy and political philosophy. In his natural philosophy, Hobbes advances mechanistic materialism, which views the universe as composed of material bodies subject to necessary scientific laws of cause and effect. Hobbes's moral philosophy includes a mechanistic account of human nature (which states that humans are natural machines subject to necessary laws) and a subjective notion of the good (according to which the 'good' is determined by each individual's desires). In his political philosophy, Hobbes advances a position known as political absolutism (according to which the only, or best, path to peace is to establish a final authority with irrevocable power). In the second section of this chapter, you were introduced to the topic of philosophical interpretation. As we have seen, there are different ways to approach a philosophical text and you must determine for yourself the approach that suits you. The third section of this chapter presented some of the basic ideas behind philosophical enquiry. Philosophy, I have suggested, is grounded in reason and rational argumentation. Thus, when you try to answer philosophical questions, you must try to use your natural power of reason to evaluate both the logic of philosophical arguments and the truth of their premises.

CHAPTER 2

HOBBES'S EPISTEMOLOGY

Epistemology is the branch of philosophy that raises questions about human knowledge: What is the source of human knowledge? What is the nature of truth? What is the proper method, if any, for acquiring knowledge? What are the limits of human reason? Hobbes spends a great deal of energy on epistemological pursuits, most likely because he recognizes the practical value of human knowledge. According to Hobbes, the application of an appropriate philosophical method leads to the discovery of 'universal truth'. Of course, if truth could be attained in the moral and political realm, where disagreements often lead to real conflict, there is no doubt that it would be welcomed. Thus, epistemology, far from being an abstract and seemingly useless endeavour, has the important practical consequence of promoting peace and prosperity in the commonwealth. The first section of this chapter summarizes the main elements of Hobbes's epistemology. As we shall see, Hobbes believed that philosophical knowledge, which originates in our sense experience of the world, has value primarily for its practical benefits. In Hobbes's view, though, sense experience alone does not give us philosophical knowledge. Instead, it is the power of human reason that allows us to move beyond mere sensation and into the realm of truth. After presenting the summary of Hobbes's epistemology, I will then present, in the second section, divergent interpretations of Hobbes's view of truth. Despite how important the concept of truth is for Hobbes, he is not entirely clear about what he means by 'truth'. In fact, as we shall see, there are good reasons to suppose that Hobbes holds two different theories of truth. After examining the evidence for the contrasting interpretations, you may decide for yourself which view of truth Hobbes 'really' holds. The chapter then concludes, in the third section, with an enquiry into the nature of truth. What does it mean to say that something is true? At first sight, the answer to this question might seem straightforward: A statement is true when it accurately describes some fact of the world. Further reflection reveals, however, that the concept of truth is anything but straightforward. After looking at three theories of truth, you may decide for yourself which theory is the most reasonable.

I. SUMMARY: HOBBES'S EPISTEMOLOGY

The Value of Knowledge

Philosophical knowledge for its own sake, Hobbes says, is not really worth the effort that it requires (*Co* 1.189). According to Hobbes, the practice of philosophy is arduous and time-consuming; in fact, if the possession of truth were its only goal, Hobbes believes, it would be better simply to abstain from it. Fortunately, numerous practical benefits accrue to knowledge to make philosophical enquiry worthwhile. In *De Corpore*, Hobbes draws an analogy between farming and reasoning to illustrate some of the practical advantages of knowledge. In days prior to systematic farming, Hobbes claims, people naturally knew how to feed themselves on acorns scattered throughout the fields. Aided by the power of reason, however, humans developed farming techniques and thereby acquired knowledge that dramatically improved their ability to sustain themselves. To produce such results, according to Hobbes, reason must be guided by a method. 'Most men wander out of the way', Hobbes says, and 'fall into error for want of method, as it were for want of sowing and planting' (*Co* 1.185). With a proper method of reasoning, in other words, errors can be avoided, knowledge attained and technological skills developed.

Knowledge not only helps us develop technological skills, it also helps us avoid disputes. The most dangerous disputes, of course, occur in the political sphere where people have very different answers to such questions as: Who should wield power? What is the best form of government? What are the respective rights and obligations of citizens and leaders? When, if ever, is civil disobedience or revolution justified? If genuine knowledge could be established in the political realm, Hobbes says, then disagreements over the answers to such questions would cease and a state of peace would ensue. It was Hobbes's aim to use a scientific method in the political sphere to acquire genuine knowledge. Without such a method, Hobbes says, people will 'do nothing but dispute and wrangle, like men that are not in their wits' (*Co* 1.185).

The Origin of Knowledge: Sensation

Hobbes claims that all ideas or conceptions, and therefore all knowledge, ultimately begins with sense perceptions of the world. 'For there is no conception in man's mind', Hobbes says, 'which has not at first totally, or by parts, been begotten upon the organs of sense' (*L* 1.85). Physical objects in the world interact with our sense organs in one of two ways: immediately or through a medium. In cases of touching and tasting, for example, objects make immediate contact with (or 'press' against, as Hobbes would say,) our sense organs. In cases of hearing, seeing and smelling, on the other hand, objects work through the mediums of light and air. In all cases of sensation, physical contact with sense organs initiates a series of internal motions that 'by the mediation of nerves, and other strings, and membranes of the body' are carried to the 'brain and heart' wherein a 'resistance, or counter-pressure' is produced (*L* 1.85). Hobbes identifies the internal motions, or 'counter pressures', with sense perceptions of colours, sounds, textures and so on. Sensible qualities of material objects, in other words, are nothing but 'diverse motions' occurring in the brain (*L* 1.86). Hobbes here adheres to what may be called a *materialist account of sensation*. According to this account, sensations are not just caused by physical motions in the brain, but are identified with them. Our experiences of such things as colours and sounds are nothing other than physical motions in the brain. Although Hobbes does not specifically distinguish between what John Locke would later call 'primary' and 'secondary' qualities, he nevertheless anticipates this distinction. The 'primary' qualities of an object are those qualities that actually belong to the object, while the 'secondary' qualities exist only in the mind. So, for example, the warmth and yellowness of the sun are secondary qualities, while the primary qualities of the sun are nothing but the minute physical particles that compose it. The secondary qualities, to put it another way, are subjective, while the primary qualities are objective.

Hobbes's account of sensation includes a *representational theory of perception*. According to this theory, our own ideas and experiences 'represent' material objects outside the mind. Every sensation, Hobbes says, is simply a 'representation or appearance of some quality or other accident' of an object (*L* 1.85). The immediate object of my experience of a chair, for example, is the collection of *my own ideas* of the chair's qualities. When I perceive the chair, I immediately experience *my own ideas* of its colour, shape, texture and so on. Imagine, for example, that your eyes are like the lens of a camera. Light from the sun reflects off a chair in the room and enters your eyes as it does though a camera lens. The light then hits the film and an image is created. After developing the film and creating a print, the photograph is an image of the original chair. When you look at the photograph, you are not immediately experiencing the chair itself, but a representation of it. In a similar manner, the image in your mind created by the action of the light on your eyes and brain is a representation of the chair.

PERPLEXING PROBLEM: THE PROBLEM OF PERCEPTION

Hobbes's representational account of perception might seem to erect a 'veil of perception' between our minds and the physical world since the immediate objects of perception are our own ideas, rather than the things themselves. The image in our minds is, like a photograph, a representation of the original object. To determine whether a photograph is an accurate representation of an object, we simply need to compare the photograph with the object itself. Imagine, however, that you can only see the photograph. How can you determine whether the photograph accurately depicts the object? According to Hobbes, the immediate objects of perception are our own ideas and conceptions. How, then, can we get outside of our own minds to compare the conception in our minds with the object itself? Hobbes considered such a question and responded that his representational theory of perception does not create a barrier between the world and the mind. The 'object of sight', properly speaking, is 'neither light nor color, but the body itself which is lucid, or enlightened, or colored' (*Co* 25.225). Hobbes here asserts that we do experience the objects themselves. Given the fact that we perceive only our own ideas, is Hobbes justified in making such a claim? Can you think of a way to help Hobbes out of this difficulty?

Imagination

Hobbes distinguishes between the immediate sensation of an object (which occurs when someone actively perceives an object) and the 'image' of an object (which lingers in the mind when the object is no longer present). Hobbes defines imagination as 'nothing but decaying sense' (*L* 2.88). The imagination, in other words, is nothing other than the motions that were originally caused by the pressure exerted by external objects. 'For after the object is removed', Hobbes says, 'or the eye shut, we still retain an image of the thing seen, though more obscure than when we see it' (*L* 2.88). For example, if you were to look at the sun and close your eyes, its image would still be in your mind. When these images become 'faded and old' they transform into 'memories' (*L* 2.89). As memories accumulate, one acquires 'experience', which is defined as 'much memory or memory of many things' (*L* 2.89). The imagination is also responsible for the images that occur in dreams (*L* 2.90). Memory, experience and dreams, then, are all mental phenomena classified under the imagination. The imagination, according to Hobbes, makes 'understanding' possible. 'The imagination that is raised in man', Hobbes says, 'by words, or other voluntary signs, is that we generally call Understanding' (*L* 2.93). It is important to note that 'understanding' is common to humans and animals since it is simply the occurrence of images in the mind. A dog understands a master's call, for example, because the master's call causes a certain idea or 'image' in the dog's mind.

Images in the mind are constantly appearing and disappearing. This 'train of imagination' Hobbes also refers to as 'mental discourse', which he divides into two types, guided or unguided (*L* 3.94). In some instances, as in dreams, our thoughts wander from one idea to the next without a 'passionate thought to govern and direct them' (*L* 3.95). Guided mental discourse, on the other hand, is 'regulated by some desire and design' (*L* 3.95). A regulated train of thoughts comes in one of two varieties. On the one hand, we may seek the causes of a given thing or event from its effects or we may seek possible effects from a particular cause. If a man loses a key, for example, 'his mind runs back from place to place, and time to time, to find where and when he had it' (*L* 3.96). In this case, the man seeks the cause of the lost key through a succession of images guided by a specific purpose. The movement could also be directed towards a future goal as when, for example, one imagines a number of different ways to spend a pay cheque. The pay cheque, in other words, might 'cause', or lead to, a number of different effects. The ability to foresee possible effects of a given cause based on prior experiences is called prudence (*L* 3.97). Since similar causes are often followed by similar effects, the more experience one has of a given type of cause and the effects it produces, the more likely one is to anticipate the actual effects of a present cause. A prudent person, then, has a considerable amount of experience with a certain type of cause and its corresponding effects and is thereby better equipped to conjecture about the future.

Prudence, although it may help one achieve a variety of goals, does not lead to certain knowledge about the future. As Hobbes explains, prudence is based on experience and one cannot draw 'universal' conclusions from experience. 'For though a man have always seen the day and night to follow one another hitherto', Hobbes says, 'yet can he not thence conclude they shall do so, or they have done so, eternally: *experience concludes nothing universally*' (*El* I.4.10). So experience does not provide one with necessary knowledge. If you drop an apple one hundred times from your hand and it falls to the earth, it is not logically necessary that it will fall to the earth the next time it is released. All reasoning about the future, or past, based upon experience, is nothing but 'conjecture'. So, to use one of Hobbes's examples, if a man were to experience a flourishing state come to ruin, he could not conclude that the same causes applied to the ruin of previous states. Such a conjecture, Hobbes says, 'has the same uncertainty almost with the conjecture of the future, both being grounded only upon experience' (*L* 3.98).

Philosophical Knowledge and Reason

Philosophical knowledge, according to Hobbes, is an acquired form of knowledge that originates in sense experience, but is not the same as sense experience. Hobbes believes that sense experience is a lower form of knowledge. In addition, other forms of 'understanding', such as prudence, are also not to be confused with philosophical knowledge even though they, too, begin with the senses. According to Hobbes, reason is the faculty responsible for acquiring philosophical knowledge. Put simply, reason is a calculating faculty that 'adds' and 'subtracts' ideas. To illustrate this, Hobbes uses an example of perceiving a man in the distance. According to this example, when you see a man very far away, you first perceive him simply as a 'body', unaware of whether he is a man, woman, animal or even an inanimate object. As the body comes closer, you realize that it is 'animated'. Finally, if this animated body reaches you and begins a conversation, you realize that it is a rational and animated body, i.e., a human being. Reason takes numerous concepts gained from experience and adds them together into one. So, for example, reason adds together 'body', 'rational' and 'animated' into the concept 'human'. Similarly, if the man were to walk away, you would first subtract the idea of rationality from the man. As he walks further away, you would then subtract the idea of animation. For Hobbes, reason carries out the subtraction and addition of any kinds of concepts or things. 'In sum', Hobbes claims, wherever there is a 'place for addition and subtraction, there is also a place for reason' (*L* 5.110–1).

Resolution and Composition

Hobbes's method for philosophical enquiry is the resolutive-compositive method, which was used by Galileo to investigate natural phenomena. Simply put, Hobbes believes that to understand a given thing properly, it must be imaginatively broken down, or 'resolved', into its 'constitutive causes', or component parts. For Hobbes, 'everything is best understood by its constitutive causes' (*Ci* Preface. 98). Resolving a body to understand it is analogous to understanding the workings of a watch by dismantling it. 'For as in a watch, or some such small engine', Hobbes says in *De Cive*, 'the matter, figure, and motion of the wheels cannot be well known, except it be taken asunder and viewed in parts' (*Ci* Preface. 98). This also relates to Hobbes's notion of reason as a 'calculating' faculty that adds and subtracts. The process of resolution, for example, is the 'subtraction' of the parts from the whole. In any case, resolution not only reveals constitutive causes, but also properties that are more 'universal' than the 'singular' things being resolved. When a particular thing is resolved, in other words, it is broken up into common properties. To use one of Hobbes's examples, imagine that you have an idea of a particular square in your mind. This square may be resolved into the following properties: plane, straight lines, equal lines and right angles. Such properties are 'more universal' than the square itself because each property belongs to other figures. Straight lines, for example, are properties of rectangles, among other things. After discovering the constitutive causes and properties of a given thing, one may use the second part of the resolutive-compositive method to 'compose' the thing from its causes (or to 'add' its properties together to create the whole). By understanding the fundamental properties of a square, for example, one can correctly construct or, as Hobbes might say, 'generate', a square. Unfortunately, when Hobbes speaks of his philosophical method, he does not always use the same descriptive terms. So, for example, he variously describes his method in terms of breaking up a 'whole' into its 'parts', discovering the 'causes' from the 'effects', and understanding the 'appearance' of something by its 'generation'. In one place, Hobbes says that philosophical knowledge is 'knowledge of effects or appearances, as we acquire by true ratiocination from the knowledge we have first of their causes or generation: And again, of such causes or generations as may be from knowing their effects' (*Co* 1.3). Thus, Hobbes says that a thing's constituent parts are identified with its 'causes', which are responsible for its 'generation'. So, in the case of the square, its various 'parts' are the 'causes' of its being 'generated'.

Scientific Demonstration

Hobbes not only wants to acquire knowledge for himself, but also to demonstrate this knowledge to others. At 40 years old, Hobbes 'fell in love' with geometry because of its power to scientifically demonstrate conclusions on the basis of self-evident or universally accepted principles.[1] John Aubrey, who included a Hobbes biography in his *Brief Lives*, describes the origin of his subject's 'love' of geometry.

> He was . . . 40 years old before he looked on geometry, which happened accidentally. Being in a gentleman's library . . . Euclid's *Elements* lay open, and 'twas the 47 *Ellibri* 1. He read the proposition. 'By G—,' said he, (he would now and then swear by way of emphasis), 'this is impossible!' So he reads the demonstration of it, which referred him back to such a proposition, which proposition he read. That referred him back to another, which he also read. *Et sic deinceps*, that at last was demonstrably convinced of the truth. This made him in love with geometry.[2]

Geometry provides the perfect model of scientific demonstration for Hobbes because it constructs arguments on the basis of universally accepted first principles or definitions.[3] An argument, philosophically speaking, is a series of propositions one of which (the 'conclusion') is logically deduced from the others (the 'premises'). The basic kind of argument for Hobbes is the 'syllogism', which consists of two premises that logically support a given conclusion. For example, from the two premises, 'all apples are fruit' and 'all fruit is nutritious', one may logically derive the conclusion 'all apples are nutritious'. For a syllogism to be 'scientific', according to Hobbes, it must have a conclusion that is both true and universal. Regarding the truth requirement, Hobbes says that 'all true ratiocination [reasoning] which takes its beginnings from true principles produces science and is true demonstration' (*Co* 6.208). The conclusions of a scientific demonstration must also be universal. A universal proposition, such as 'all apples are nutritious', permits no exceptions and so captures a characteristic of the entire class of apples. One positive feature of scientific knowledge, according to Hobbes, is precisely this ability to transcend particular situations by making universal claims. A scientific demonstration, then, is a syllogism that starts with true and universal propositions and, on the basis of these, validly deduces conclusions with the same characteristics.

PERPLEXING PROBLEM: THE PROBLEM OF SCIENCE

In *Leviathan*, Hobbes provides two definitions of scientific knowledge. In the first case, he defines science as factual knowledge of causes and effects. In the second case, he defines science as 'conditional' knowledge of 'affirmations' (statements). For example, given that I know what 'circle' means, I can make the following affirmation that 'if something is a circle, then it is round'. In this case, scientific knowledge simply seems to be a matter of knowing the definitions of words. Compare these two passages from *Leviathan*:

> Science is the knowledge of consequences and dependence of one fact upon another by which . . . we know how to do something else when we will . . . because when we see how anything comes about, upon what causes, and by what manner, when the like causes come into our power, we see how to make it produce the like effects (*L* 5.115).

Science . . . is conditional, as when we know that, 'If the figure shown be a circle, then any straight line through the center shall divide it into two equal parts.' And this is the knowledge required in a philosopher (*L* 9.147).

Are these two passages consistent with each other? How might Hobbes respond to the accusation that he has two different conceptions of science?

Truth

For Hobbes, truth is a characteristic of propositions in which one 'name' of the proposition 'signifies' or 'comprehends' another. A 'name' is a word used either as a 'mark' or a 'sign' of an idea or a conception in our minds. A 'mark' is a word that functions as a mnemonic device to recall an idea to mind. For example, I may use the word 'dog' to recall the idea of a dog. A 'sign', on the other hand, is a word used to communicate one's thoughts to others. For example, I may use 'dog' to 'signify' to you that I am thinking of a dog. Names, Hobbes says, have different levels of signification insofar as they 'comprehend' more or fewer things. 'Proper' names, for example, signify our ideas of specific individuals, while 'common' names signify our ideas of groups. Common names, when they signify all individuals of a given class, are 'universal' names. 'Peter Piper' is a proper name because it signifies an individual, while 'man' is both universal and common because it signifies all members of a group. Some kinds of names, in other words, have a greater scope than others. True propositions are those in which the subject term is included within the scope of the predicate term. As Hobbes says:

> When two names are joined into a consequence or affirmation, such as *a man is a living creature* or *if he be a man, he is a living creature*, if the latter name *living creature* signifies all that the former name *man* signifies, then the affirmation or consequence is *true*, otherwise, it is *false*' (*L* 4.104-5).

In other words, when I say that 'man is a living creature', I am saying that the name 'living creature' is a broader term that, by definition, includes 'man'.

For Hobbes, truth is a linguistic characteristic belonging to propositions. In fact, it is the linguistic character of truth that makes scientific knowledge possible. To illustrate this, Hobbes points out that a person without language may discover that the three angles of a particular triangle are equal to two right angles, but 'if another triangle be shown him different in shape from the former, he cannot know without a new labor whether the three angles of that are also equal to the same' (L 4.103). A person with speech, however, can 'mark' this truth with the statement that the 'three angles of a triangle equal two right angles'. Language, Hobbes says, 'delivers us from the labor of the mind' and 'makes that which was found true *here*, and *now*, to be true in *all times* and *places*' (L 4.104). So scientific truth is made possible through language because names allow us not only to mark and remember our discoveries, but also to communicate them to others.

Geometry and Physics

In *De Corpore*, Hobbes presents the main elements of his natural philosophy, including his ideas on geometry and physics. The two different sciences reveal different kinds or levels of knowledge. Geometry, Hobbes says, considers the concepts of 'motion and magnitude by themselves in the abstract' (Co 24.386). Physics, on the other hand, studies the 'motions and magnitudes of the bodies which are parts of the world, real and existent' (Co 24.386). In Hobbes's view, geometry is a science that demonstrates the truth of its conclusions, while physics remains in the realm of hypotheses. The reason for this difference, according to Hobbes, is the fact that the principles of geometry are definitions that are accepted as true. With these principles in place, one can then demonstrate the truth of conclusions drawn from these principles. The principles of physics, however, are discovered through experience; they are not created by us, but are put into the world by God. These principles, Hobbes says, 'are not such as we make and pronounce in general terms, as definitions; but such as being placed in things themselves by the Author of Nature are by us observed in them' (Co 25.288). According to Hobbes, we are not allowed to draw any universally true conclusions on the basis of observation. Even if we observe that night and day have always followed each other, he says, we cannot conclude that it will always be this way since 'experience concludes nothing universally' (El I.4.10). Physics 'depends upon hypotheses, which, unless we know them to be true, it is impossible for us to demonstrate that those causes, which I have there explicated, are the true causes' (*Co* 30.531). Thus, the conclusions of physics cannot be demonstrated as true since we cannot know if the primary principles are true. Conclusions in geometry, however, are capable of demonstrable proof because the principles are 'constructed by us'.

PERPLEXING PROBLEM: THE PROBLEM OF EXPERIENCE

Hobbes believes he has established a *scientific* political philosophy grounded on *true* principles. Regardless of what truth actually means in this case, it is clear that his political philosophy is supposed to be true. In many places, however, Hobbes claims that the principles of his political philosophy are known by experience. For example, in *De Cive*, Hobbes 'sets down for a principle by experience known to all men and denied by none, to wit, that the dispositions of men are naturally such, that except they be restrained by some coercive power, every man will dread and distrust each other' (*Ci* Preface. 99). In the *Elements of Law,* Hobbes presents a principle that is the 'true and only foundation of such [a political] science' *(El* Epistle). Hobbes then says he is 'not intending to take any principle upon trust, but only to put men in mind of what they know already, or may know by their experience' (*El* I.1.2). Hobbes says his political philosophy is 'grounded on its own principles sufficiently known by experience' (*Ci* Preface. 103). The foundational principles of his political philosophy, then, are supposedly known by experience. Experience, however, cannot be the basis for universal truth claims. Herein lies the problem of experience. If political philosophy is grounded on empirical principles known by experience and experience cannot draw out any universally true conclusions, then Hobbes's political philosophy cannot draw out any universally true conclusions. Thus, Hobbes's political philosophy cannot be a genuine science. Hobbes's view of experience, in other words, seems to be inconsistent with the claim that his political philosophy is a science. Is Hobbes truly inconsistent in this matter? Can you find a way to interpret Hobbes to avoid this problem?

Empiricism and Rationalism

Philosophers of the sixteenth and seventeenth centuries are generally classified as either empiricists or rationalists when it comes to their theories of knowledge. Empiricists believe that knowledge ultimately begins in, and is confirmed by, experience. John Locke claimed that the human mind begins as a *tabula rasa*, or blank slate, which is imprinted by our experiences. There is no knowledge without some sort of empirical confirmation. Rationalists, on the other hand, believe knowledge is found through rational reflection of one's ideas without confirmation of experience. René Descartes, for example, was a rationalist who recognized that 'I think therefore I am' was a truth immediately available to reason without empirical confirmation. To know that I exist, I do not have to use my senses; I simply recognize the truth of this claim as I would the claim that 'something can and cannot exist at the same time'. In any case, from the foundational truth that he exists, Descartes attempted to derive other truths through logical reasoning. Turning to Hobbes, we might say that he is both an empiricist and a rationalist. He is an empiricist insofar as he believes knowledge ultimately begins with sense experience, but he also believes that genuine knowledge relies on first premises that are universal and true. According to Hobbes, experience itself cannot be the basis for drawing out universally true claims. For example, from the fact that every crow I have experienced is black, I cannot justifiably claim that 'all crows are black'. In such cases, then, Hobbes's position seems to be closer to rationalism.

II. INTERPRETATION: WHAT IS HOBBES'S THEORY OF TRUTH?

In the previous section, I presented a summary of Hobbes's epistemology based on *my reading* of his texts. You may read the same texts and find a different Hobbes. In this section, we will explore just one area of scholarly disagreement in Hobbes's epistemology, his view of truth. According to one interpretation, Hobbes holds a 'conventional theory of truth' according to which the truth of propositions depends upon human convention and agreement over word usage:[4] to say that a statement is true is simply to say that people have agreed to it. According to a different interpretation, Hobbes accepts a 'correspondence theory of truth'. According to this view, the truth of propositions is determined by their degree of 'correspondence' to reality.[5] To say that a statement is true means that it reveals some objective fact about reality. In this section, I will make some introductory comments about these two interpretations. We will then look at specific passages from Hobbes's texts in an effort to find the best interpretation of his view of truth.

The Conventional Theory of Truth

There is a good amount of evidence to support the interpretation that Hobbes accepts a conventional theory of truth. The bulk of this evidence rests on Hobbes's claim that truth describes a relationship between the names of a proposition and not a relationship between names and the world. As Hobbes says, 'truth consists in speech and not in the things spoken of' (*Co* 3.35). A true proposition does not describe some fact about the world, but simply reveals something about the way we use words. For example, if 'all apples are fruit' is a true proposition, this does not mean that all apples in the world are fruit. Instead, it simply means that we sometimes use the words 'fruit' and 'apple' to signify the same idea. Hobbes, as we have seen, says that a name is a 'mark' or 'sign' of a *conception*; a name does not mark or signify the thing itself, but simply our ideas of it. The word 'apple', for example, marks or signifies my conception of an apple, not the apple that exists in the real world. Truth, then, does not describe a relationship between conceptions of things and the things themselves, but only a relationship between conceptions and words.

Further evidence for the conventional theory of truth in Hobbes is found in his claim that names are 'arbitrarily' assigned to various conceptions by an act of will. Hobbes says, for example, that a 'name or appellation therefore is the voice of a man, arbitrarily imposed, for a mark to bring to his mind some conception concerning the thing on which it is imposed' (*El* I.5.2). If names are arbitrarily imposed, does it not follow that propositions, which are made up of names, are created by an act of will? And, if this is the case, does it not also follow that the truth of propositions depends simply on the way we use words? In *De Corpore*, Hobbes seems to answer both of these questions affirmatively when he says that the 'first truths were arbitrarily made by those that first of all imposed names upon things or received them from the impositions of others' (*Co* 3.36). In this case, then, the truth of propositions is based simply upon human convention or agreement.

The Correspondence Theory of Truth

Despite the explicit evidence to the contrary, there is also good reason to believe that Hobbes accepts a correspondence theory of truth. According to this theory, true propositions actually corres- pond to, or describe, reality. Thus, if 'all apples are fruit' is true, then all apples really are fruit. The bulk of the evidence for believing Hobbes accepts a correspondence theory consists in the fact that the success of his political philosophy requires that it is 'true' in the sense that it accurately describes reality. Hobbes, as we have seen, wants to present a political philosophy that could resolve conflicts by provid- ing the 'truth' about political matters. So Hobbes wants to show that some political views are right and some are wrong. If truth is simply a matter of convention, then, technically speaking, any political views can be true as long as people agree to the terminology. It seems unlikely, however, that Hobbes believes his political philosophy is true simply by definition. As was briefly mentioned in the first chapter, Hobbes's scientific demonstration of his political philoso- phy is supposedly grounded upon true, indisputable premises. More specifically, Hobbes says his demonstration is grounded on a truth about human nature: humans, if they are to get along peacefully, must be coerced into behaving lawfully. 'In the first place', Hobbes says, 'I set down for a principle, by experience known to all men and denied by none, to wit, that the dispositions of men are naturally such that except they be restrained through fear of some coercive power, every man will distrust and dread each other' (*Ci* Preface. 99). In this case, Hobbes implies that certain principles of human nature are true because they genuinely describe the fact of the matter. Humans, *in reality*, are self-interested beings who need a powerful force to keep them in check. A strong government, *in reality*, is needed for peace and prosperity. Hobbes's political philosophy, *in reality*, describes the truth about political matters. It is hard to imagine that Hobbes did not believe that the truths of his philoso- phy accurately described reality.

Primary Passages to Consider

Does Hobbes hold a conventional theory of truth or a correspond- ence theory of truth? To answer this question, one should further examine his texts, consider his intentions, imagine possible responses if he were made aware of the inconsistencies in his thought and determine which theory has a better fit with the textual evidence. Perhaps Hobbes does not hold either theory of truth, but accepts an alternative. In any case, I present and comment upon important primary passages in order to help you develop your own interpretation. Passages 1–3 suggest that knowing the truth is simply a matter of grasping 'principles' or 'definitions' that have been *accepted* as true, but do these passages definitely confirm that truth, for Hobbes, is exclusively a matter of human agreement? Is there any evidence in these passages to suggest that Hobbes might still hold that true statements reflect the way the world really is? Passages 4–6, on the other hand, support the view that truth involves revealing aspects of reality. Are these passages incompatible with the first three? Is there a way to interpret Hobbes so that his views are consistent?

Comments and Questions for Passage 1

The following passage suggests that errors are made when we use names in novel and unconventional ways. If, for example, I refer to the 'sun' as the 'moon', and then claim that the 'moon is larger than the earth', it seems that my statement would be false because I have departed from the accepted definitions of 'sun' and 'moon'. Do you think Hobbes really believes that falsity arises solely from misusing words? Can you find any evidence to claim that truth requires more than proper word usage?

Passage 1

This kind of error only deserves the name of *falsity*, as arising not from sense, nor from the things themselves, but from pronouncing rashly; for names have their constitution, not from the species of things, but from the will and consent of men. And hence it comes to pass, that men pronounce falsely, by their own negligence, in departing from such appellations as are agreed upon, and are not deceived neither by the things, nor by the sense; for they do not perceive that the thing they see is called sun, but they give it that name from their own will and agreement (*Co* 5.56).

Comments and Questions for Passage 2

In Passage 2, Hobbes reaffirms that truth is a characteristic of propositions where the subject term is contained within the scope of the predicate term. He further suggests that truth is a matter of knowing 'definitions' that have been 'settled'. In geometry, Hobbes says, humans begin by agreeing upon primary principles or definitions. Hobbes does not explain why humans might 'settle' upon one definition over another. Does this lack of an explanation indicate anything to you?

> Passage 2
> When two names are joined together into a consequence [a statement] or affirmation, as thus, *A man is a living creature*, or thus, *if he be a man, he is a living creature*, if the later name *living creature* signify all that the former name *man* signifies, then the affirmation, or consequence, is *true*; otherwise it is *false*. For *true* and *false* are attributes of speech, not of things. And where speech is not, there is neither truth nor falsehood . . . Seeing then that truth consists in the right ordering of names in our affirmations, a man that seeks precise truth had need to remember what every name he uses stands for and to place it accordingly, or else he will find himself entangled in words, as a bird in lime twigs; the more he struggles, the more he is belimed. And therefore in geometry, which is the only science that it has pleased God hitherto to bestow on mankind, men begin at the settling of their words, which settling of significations, they call *definitions* and place them at the beginning of their reckoning (*L* 4.104–5).

Comments and Questions for Passage 3

The following passage is taken from an objection written by Hobbes to an argument of René Descartes. Hobbes's main point in the objection is to show that there is a difference between having an idea of something and the rational process of inferring that something exists on the basis of an idea. In the process of making his objection, Hobbes seems to confirm the view that truth does not reveal anything about the nature of things, but is simply a characteristic of names. In his response to Hobbes's objection, Descartes raises the following two questions: 'Who doubts that a Frenchman and a German can reason about the same things, despite the words that they think of are completely different?' and 'For if he [Hobbes] admits that the words signify something, why will he not allow that our reasoning deals with this some-thing which is signified, rather than merely with words?'[6] Given your knowledge of Hobbes's views of word usage and sig-nification, how do you think he would respond to Descartes's questions?

Passage 3

Now, what shall we say if it turns out that reasoning is simply the joining together and linking of names and labels by means of the word 'is'? It would follow that the inferences in our reasoning tell us nothing at all about the nature of things, but merely tell us about the labels applied to them; that is, all we can infer is whether or not we are combining the names of things in accordance with the arbitrary conventions which we have laid down in respect of their meaning.[7]

Comments and Questions for Passage 4

In Passage 4, Hobbes provides definitions of 'place' and 'motion'. Interestingly, Hobbes implies that his definitions are the 'true' ones. In other words, these definitions are not agreed upon. In contrast to the previous three passages, then, this passage seems to say that there are right and wrong definitions and, therefore, that definitions are not simply true or false by agreement. This passage may be used to support the interpretation that Hobbes does not hold a conventional view of truth, but a correspondence view. Is this the best interpretation of the passage? Is Hobbes necessarily implying that his definitions accurately capture what 'place' and 'motion' really are?

Passage 4

For example, he that has a true conception of place cannot be ignorant of this definition, *place is that space which is possessed or filled adequately by some body*; and so, he that conceives *motion* aright cannot but know that *motion is the privation of one place, and the acquisition of another* (*Co* 1.6).

Comments and Questions for Passage 5

Passage 5 has also been used as evidence for a correspondence theory of truth in Hobbes. In this passage, Hobbes claims that previous political writers have consistently been at odds with each other because they have not been able to make a science out of politics. What is needed is a method, as in mathematics, that begins with true and indisputable principles. Although he does not, in this passage, specifically reveal the principles of his political philosophy, Hobbes clearly states that his principles are the 'true and only foundation' for a political science. Does this suggest that Hobbes's principles are more than just conventional definitions? Is he necessarily advocating a correspondence view of truth?

Passage 5
[T]hey that have written of justice and policy in general, do all invade each other and themselves with contradiction. To reduce this doctrine [political philosophy] to the rules and infallibility of reason, there is no way, but first to put such principles down for a foundation, as passion not mistrusting, may not seek to displace; and afterward to build thereon the truth of cases in the law of nature (which hitherto have been built in the air) by degrees, till the whole be inexpugnable. Now (my Lord) the principles fit for such a foundation, are those which I have heretofore acquainted with your Lordship withal in private discourse and which by your command I have here put into method. To examine cases thereby between sovereign and subject, I leave to them that shall find leisure and encouragement thereto. For my part, I present this to your Lordship for the true and only foundation of such science. For the style, it is therefore the worse because I was forced to consult when I was writing, more with logic than with rhetoric. But for the doctrine, it is not slightly proved and the conclusions thereof are of such a nature, as, for want of them, government and peace have been nothing else to this day, but mutual fear (*El* Epistle).

Comments and Questions for Passage 6

Passage 6 provides more evidence for a correspondence view of truth. In this passage, Hobbes suggests that he uses the method of resolution in his political philosophy to understand the commonwealth. This resolution reveals to him the fundamental principle that humans need to be coerced into lawful behaviour if they are to live peacefully with one another. This principle, which is 'known by experience' and 'denied by none', is the foundation of Hobbes's science of politics. Does Hobbes necessarily imply that this principle is true in the sense that it accurately describes the reality of human nature?

Passage 6
Concerning my method, I thought it not sufficient to use a plain and evident style in what I have to deliver, except I took my beginning from the very matter of civil government and thence proceeded to its

generation and form and the first beginning of justice. For everything is best understood according to its constitutive causes. For as in a watch, or some such small engine, the matter, figure, and motion of the wheels cannot be well known, except it be taken asunder and viewed in parts; so to make a more curious search into the rights of states and duties of subjects, it is necessary, I say, not to take them asunder, but yet that they may be considered as if they were dissolved; that is, that we rightly understand what the quality of human nature is, in what matters it is, in what not, fit to make up a civil government and how much men must be agreed amongst themselves that intend to grow up in a well-grounded state. Having therefore followed this kind of method, in the first place I set down for a principle, by experience known to all men and denied by none, to wit, that the dispositions of men are naturally such, that except they be restrained through fear of some coercive power, every man will distrust and dread each other; and as by natural right he may, so by necessity he will be forced to make use of the strength he hath, toward the preservation of himself (*Ci* Preface. 98–9).

III. ENQUIRY: WHAT IS THE NATURE OF TRUTH?

While the task of interpretation is important, it should not overshadow the task of enquiry. Whatever Hobbes's actual position on truth, we must also ourselves enquire into the nature of truth; we must not only ask what Hobbes's view of truth is, but whether his view is right. Such an enquiry raises the following questions: What are the strengths and weaknesses of the two positions on truth thus far discussed? Is one view philosophically stronger? Are there other options and, if so, are they philosophically stronger? These questions will now be explored and it will be up to you to judge which view of truth is the best.

Correspondence View of Truth

The correspondence view of truth, as we have seen, claims that a statement is true if and only if it corresponds to, or accurately describes, reality. The main strength of this view is found in our natural sense of what it means to say something is 'true'. For example, it seems natural to say the 'moon revolves around the earth' is true because, *in reality*, the moon *does* revolve around the earth. A further strength is the assumption that there is an 'objective' fact of the matter which, when properly known, leads to agreement among conflicting parties. Practically speaking, as Hobbes himself intimated, truth in this sense could result in numerous practical benefits, the most important of which is political stability. If there were an objectively true answer to the question of what form of government is the best, humans might be able to live in peace and prosperity. Of course, many of us doubt whether truth can be found in the social sciences. Yet, it seems hard to deny that natural science has not progressed towards the *truth*, given that technological advances based on such science seem to rely upon our ability to understand the reality of the natural world. Our ability to build and successfully fly aeroplanes, for example, seems to rely upon the *real truth* about aerodynamics. Does not such technological knowledge confirm that, to say the least, we have grasped the truth about some aspects of reality?

At first glance, the correspondence theory of truth seems to have a lot going for it. Further reflection, however, gives rise to some interesting and difficult philosophical questions. First, to which, or to whose, reality does the truth correspond? It is commonly recognized that individuals experience reality differently. Where one person sees a red apple, for instance, someone else might see a green apple. What, then, is the true colour of the apple? Perhaps, as Hobbes says, colour does not really belong to the perceived object, but is simply an experience in the mind of the perceiver. In this case, then, the 'truth' is that the apple has no colour at all. Going even further, we might say that apples are simply collections of tiny physical particles in motion. But, if this is the case, then an apple does not have any of the characteristics normally attributed to it. So in truth, apples are not red, not round, not crunchy, not sweet and so on. It follows from this that almost none of the truths we accept on a daily basis corresponds to reality. A further difficulty arises from the fact that some statements seem to be true even if they do not correspond to reality. For example, is it not true to say a 'figure with twenty million sides has more than ten sides'? What if there is no *real* figure with this many sides? Isn't the statement true anyway? These questions present serious difficulties for adherents of the correspondence view of truth.

Conventional View of Truth

The conventional view of truth, as explicitly advocated by Hobbes, suggests that truth is simply a characteristic of language.

A statement is true if there is a specific kind of relationship between its names. According to Hobbes, if the subject is 'comprehended' by the predicate, then the statement is true. For example, 'all apples are fruit' is true because the word 'fruit' includes, or comprehends, the word 'apples' insofar as anything that is called an apple is also called a fruit. So, truth is not based on a relationship between the words 'apple' and 'fruit' or between real apples and fruit. Instead, truth is determined simply by the meaning of the terms. An apple, by definition, is a kind of fruit. Because this theory holds that truth is linguistic, then, it can escape some of the problems associated with the correspondence view. For example, there is no question about how true statements correspond to reality because, to repeat Hobbes's words, 'truth consists in speech and not in the things spoken of' (*Co* 3.35). It is true that an 'apple is round', in other words, if we agree as to the meanings of 'apple' and 'round'. In addition, it is true that 'a million-sided figure has more than ten sides' because we know that 'a million-sided figure' is, by definition, a 'figure with more than ten sides'.

The obvious weakness of the conventional theory of truth seems to be that it makes truth a completely subjective matter. Is it true that the moon revolves around the earth simply because we agree to it? In addition, why would people agree to this claim if it did not, in some way, actually describe reality itself? If we agreed that $2+4=7$, would that make it true? There seems to be, in other words, a complete lack of objectivity in truth claims according to this theory. The conventional theory of truth also seems to be self-defeating because, if it were 'true', it would not have any objective validity. One might ask, for example, whether the conventional theory is itself 'true'. If it is true, then it seems to be true simply for those who agree to it. If it is false, then obviously it is not the right theory of truth. Another major weakness of the conventional theory of truth is its failure to provide a good reason for accepting a given statement as true. It seems, in other words, to make the acceptance of a truth claim an arbitrary decision based on pure whim. Why should I accept as true the statement 'the moon revolves around the earth'? The conventional theory provides no answer to this question.

The Coherence Theory of Truth

The coherence theory of truth claims that we should accept a statement as true because it 'coheres' with our system of beliefs and experiences. The theory suggests that we give up on the notion of 'correspondence to reality' because it does not account for many commonly accepted 'truths', such as those found in mathematics and geometry. Instead, adherents of this theory suggest that we should focus on the reasons why we hold beliefs. Similar to the conventional theory of truth, the coherence theory suggests that truth is really a matter of acceptance or agreement. It improves upon the conventional theory by providing a reason to accept a given statement, namely, that it 'fits' with our other beliefs. The 'moon revolves around the earth' should be accepted as true because it fits in with other beliefs that we have, e.g. that the moon is a celestial body, that there is a gravitational attraction between the earth and the moon, that the moon is smaller than the earth and so on. In addition, this theory suggests that we also use our experiences to accept truth claims. According to our experience, apples are red (in most cases), so it is acceptable for us to believe that 'apples are red'. If, however, we have good reasons to deny our experiences, then we may not accept certain statements on the basis of experience. If, for example, I believe I am colourblind, then perhaps I would accept the claim that apples are red, even though I personally do not see them as red. The coherence theory of truth changes the question from 'do my statements correspond to reality?' to 'what reasons do I have for accepting statements as true?'

The coherence theory of truth also has strengths and weaknesses. It shares one of its strengths with the conventional theory of truth; it avoids the whole problematic issue of trying to determine the meaning of 'correspondence to reality'. It has the additional strength, however, of providing a reason to 'accept' certain truths. The conventional theory of truth, as we have seen, does not provide any reason why one statement should be accepted as true over another. For the coherence theory, a statement or belief should be accepted if it fits with all of our other beliefs. Its greatest weakness is that it may not provide a good criterion for deciding between two belief systems that are inconsistent with each other, but internally coherent. It seems that I could, for example, have a consistent and coherent view of the universe that claims my experience of the world is controlled by aliens. Is coherence the only condition for truth? If so, then it seems difficult to choose between different belief systems.

The Pragmatic Theory of Truth

The pragmatic theory of truth, like the coherence theory, suggests that we focus on the reasons for accepting statements as true, rather than on trying to determine whether statements accurately describe reality. The criterion for this theory, however, is not just *coherence*, but *practicality*. For the pragmatists, we should accept beliefs as true primarily because they prove to be useful. Obviously, truths derived from our common experiences are very useful because they allow us to communicate with each other and to navigate through the world. The truth about gravity, for example, allows us to predict that objects will fall when unsupported. 'The box will fall if you let it go' is an accepted truth that works well for us. Does this mean that gravity *really* exists? For the pragmatist, this is a useless question that need not be raised. Of course, all evidence of our experiences points to the existence of a gravitational force, so accepting it as true is perfectly reasonable. The pragmatist theory of truth shares the same basic strengths and weaknesses of the coherence theory. It does, however, provide an additional reason for accepting certain statements as true. So, if one is stuck between two inconsistent belief systems, the pragmatist would tell you to choose the one that is most practically useful. Whether this is a satisfying answer, I leave to you to decide.

CONCLUSION

In this chapter, the summary of Hobbes's epistemology revealed that he holds the following beliefs about knowledge and truth: (1) the value of knowledge lies primarily in its pragmatic application; (2) the origin of knowledge is sense experience; (3) philosophical knowledge is acquired by an act of reason; (4) the appropriate method of philosophical investigation involves the resolutive-compositive method; (5) scientific demonstration must be grounded on universal and true propositions; and (6) truth is a characteristic of propositions. After the summary, an interpretative conflict over Hobbes's theory of truth was presented. As we have seen, there seems to be evidence that Hobbes adheres to two incompatible theories of truth: the conventional theory of truth and the correspondence theory of truth. The last section of the chapter initiated an enquiry into the nature of truth by presenting four competing theories of truth: the correspondence theory of truth (true propositions reveal facts about the world); the conventional theory of truth (true propositions are made true by agreement); the pragmatic theory of truth (true propositions are useful); and the coherence theory of truth (true propositions are those which cohere to your other beliefs).

CHAPTER 3

HOBBES'S METAPHYSICS

Metaphysics is the branch of philosophy that raises fundamental questions about the nature of reality and human existence: What is the nature of reality? Is reality physical, spiritual or both? What is the relationship between the mind and the body? Are human actions freely chosen or are they determined by causal factors beyond a person's direct control? Are human beings selfish by nature? In this chapter, we will investigate Hobbes's answers to numerous metaphysical questions. For many philosophers, including Hobbes, metaphysical ideas have a dramatic impact on their views in other areas of philosophy. For example, if we know that human beings are selfish by nature, this would likely affect our view of the best form of political settlement. Or, to take another example, if philosophical reflection leads us to the metaphysical conclusions that the human soul does not exist and that there is no afterlife, this would probably have an impact on our opinions concerning the value of this life. The first section of this chapter summarizes the main elements of Hobbes's metaphysics. As we shall see, Hobbes adheres to a materialist view that regards reality as nothing other than physical bodies moving according to strict scientific laws. Even human behaviour, Hobbes says, falls within the framework of the causality that rules over the natural world. Furthermore, human beings are ultimately nothing but material bodies whose minds or souls are also material. In the second section, competing interpretations of Hobbes's egoism will be presented. It will be questioned whether Hobbes adheres to psychological egoism, a philosophical position that holds all human actions to be selfishly motivated. As might be expected, there are two different answers to this question, both of which have some basis in Hobbes's texts. In the third section, we will enquire into the nature of the mind. Is the mind a physical entity, or does it exist in its own realm? To start the enquiry into these questions, I will present René Descartes's view of the mind and body relationship. Descartes was a contemporary of Hobbes who disagreed with Hobbes's materialist view of the mind. After looking at both views, you may decide for yourself whose position is stronger.

I. SUMMARY: HOBBES'S METAPHYSICS

Mechanistic Materialism

Hobbes's thinking on the nature of reality was greatly influenced by the scientific outlook of his day. Galileo and other scientists replaced Aristotle's 'teleological' model of the universe with a new mechanical model. Aristotle explains the motions or changes of the universe by reference to 'final causes'. A final cause is the end point towards which things aim. According to Aristotle's model, every natural being has a 'telos', or purpose, towards which it strives. 'Heavy bodies', to use one of Hobbes's examples of Aristotle's causes, 'fall downwards out of an appetite to rest and to conserve their nature in that place which is most proper for them' (*L* 2.87). Inanimate objects, in other words, return to earth when released in the air because their natural state is one of rest. Hobbes believes this model of natural movement involves a false attribution of human desires to natural objects. 'For men measure not only other men, but all other things, by themselves', Hobbes says, 'and because they find themselves subject after motion to pain and lassitude, they think every thing else grows *wary* of motion and seeks repose of its own accord' (*L* 2.87). The mechanical model, by contrast, looks at the natural world as if it were a mechanism, rather than a teleological or intentional system. According to this model, movement and change are the result of efficient causality, which is closer to the meaning of causality today. The efficient causes of a given event, to put it simply, are the prior conditions and forces that cause it to happen. For example, gravity is an efficient cause of a stone falling to earth when released. According to Hobbes, all things in the universe, including humans, are basically machines designed by the great 'artificer', i.e. God. While the Aristotelian model uses human motives to understand the movements of natural objects, Hobbes's model uses the machine to understand human life. 'For what is the *heart*',

Hobbes asks, 'but a *spring*; and the *nerves* but so many *strings*; and the *joints*, but so many *wheels*, giving motion to the whole body, such as was intended by the Artificer?' (*L* Intro. 81). In addition, Hobbes's mechanical model (which was shared by other contemporary philosophers such as Descartes) includes the idea that motion, rather than rest, is the natural state of beings. 'When a body is once in motion', Hobbes says, 'it moves (unless something else hinders it) eternally' (*L* 2.88). Hobbes's mechanical model is accompanied by a materialist view of the universe; a materialist argues that only corporeal bodies exist. The universe is simply the 'aggregate of all bodies'? according to Hobbes, and therefore 'there is no real part thereof that is not also body' (*L* 34.428). The idea of incorporeal substances, such as souls or spirits, is completely incomprehensible to Hobbes because substances are corporeal by definition. 'Substance and body signify the same thing', he says, 'and therefore *substance incorporeal* are words, which when they are joined together, destroy one another, as if a man should say, an *incorporeal body*' (*L* 34.428). Reality, according to Hobbes, is nothing but bodies in motion.

Nominalism

Hobbes adheres to a philosophical doctrine known as nominalism, which claims that reality is composed only of individual entities.[1] This doctrine is best understood by contrasting it with the philosophical positions of realism and conceptualism (it should be noted that 'realism' has other philosophical meanings that are not related to this specific type of realism). According to realism, common properties, such as blueness, have a real existence. For example, the realist would claim that two blue objects share the common property *blueness*, which is a property that genuinely exists. The realist also claims that relationships between objects genuinely exist. For example, if object A is larger than object B and object C is larger than object D, then the relationship between A and B is the same existing relationship as that between C and D. Realists are generally divided into Platonists (who believe universal properties or relationships exist independently of particular objects) and Aristotelians (who believe universals exist within particular objects). In both cases, the fundamental claim of the realist is the same: universals exist. Conceptualism, by contrast, claims that universals only have existence within the mind. For example, the universal term 'dog' refers to a concept in one's mind that is constructed by abstracting common qualities from the experience of numerous dogs. In other words, a conceptualist denies the existence of real essences and accepts the presence of a universal concept in the mind. Nominalists, in contrast to both realists and conceptualists, claim that universals simply do not exist. Although we may use universal names, such as 'dog', there is still no such thing as a 'universal dog', in reality or in the mind. A universal name, according to the nominalist, does not refer to a universal entity, but a collection of individuals. The word 'dog', for example, does not refer to a 'universal' dog, but to the collection of all individual dogs. Hobbes criticizes realist philosophers who claim that universal names refer to real things.

> This universality of one name to many things has been the cause that men think that the things themselves are universal and do seriously contend that besides Peter and John, and all the rest of the men that are, have been, or shall be in the world, there is yet someone else that we call man, viz., man in general, deceiving themselves by taking the universal, or the general appellation, for the thing it signifies (*El* I.5.6).

Hobbes also rejects conceptualism when he criticizes philosophers who 'say the idea of anything is universal, as if there could be in the mind an image of a man, which were not the image of some one man, but a man simply, which is impossible; for every idea is one and of one thing' (*Co* 5.60). If I have the idea of 'man' in my mind, in other words, I do not have an image in my mind of mankind in general, but a specific image of an individual man. 'This word *universal*', Hobbes says, 'is never the name of anything existent in nature, nor of any idea or phantasm formed in the mind, but always the name of some word or name' (*Co* 2.20).

PERPLEXING PROBLEM: THE PROBLEM OF 'SIMILITUDES'

According to Hobbes's nominalism, everything that exists is individual and singular. Despite this claim, Hobbes seems to admit that certain things share common qualities or 'similitudes'. In *Leviathan*, for example, Hobbes says 'one universal name is imposed on many things for their similitude in some quality or other accident'

(*L* 4.103). So, the universal word 'blue' could be applied to the blue chair and the blue table because both of them are blue. According to one Hobbes scholar, this means that a 'common name gets extended to new objects not arbitrarily, but in accordance with such objective resemblances'.[2] The problem is that the existence of common properties like 'blueness' seems to be inconsistent with the claim that everything is individual and singular. If, for example, 'blue' is applied to two objects, then they have the *same property*. But if nominalism is true, how can the *same property* exist in two different places? Is there any way around this problem for Hobbes?

The Mechanics of Human Behaviour

Hobbes uses a mechanical model to explain not only the various motions and changes of the natural world, but also involuntary and voluntary human actions.[3] Involuntary actions, such as the circulation of the blood through the body, occur without thought or reflection. These 'vital motions', Hobbes says, continue uninterrupted throughout life. Voluntary actions, which he also refers to as 'animal motions', are preceded by an intention in the mind. These motions are the final result of a long chain of motions that begins with sense experience of the world. As seen in Chapter 2, Hobbes says that external objects react with our sense organs and cause 'fancies' (or conceptions) in the mind. These fancies, Hobbes says, eventually lead us to have certain 'endeavours', which are the 'small beginnings of motion, within the body of man, before they appear in walking, speaking, striking, and other visible actions' (*L* 6.119). Endeavours are basically inclinations towards or away from objects.[4] They are divided into two types: appetites and aversions. An appetite leads one to desire a particular object and an aversion leads one to avoid it. Imagine that I enter a room and look at a bowl of apples on the table. At first, I will simply see the apples and have an image of them in my mind. Next, the experience of the apples gives rise to the idea of how sweet apples taste. This idea, in turn, leads to a feeling of hunger. At this point, an appetite for an apple arises and I desire to have one. Finally, I act on this desire and proceed to take an apple from the bowl and to eat it. In this case, the experience of the apples caused me to desire one. Of course, the same experience may lead you to have an aversion if, for example, you do not like the taste of apples.

'Deliberation' is the process of deciding to act upon appetites and aversions. When a person deliberates, Hobbes says, he or she weighs the various appetites and aversions to determine what act, given the specific circumstances, will produce the most 'good' for the individual concerned (L 6.127). Imagine that I am at a party and am starting to feel very hungry. The host of the party is only serving cake, biscuits and ice-cream. When I first see the foods, I have an appetite for the biscuits and see them as 'good'. Next, however, the idea arises that I should be eating more than sweets. I then think of the negative consequences when I eat only sweets for dinner. I begin to think it would be 'good' for me if I do not eat anything. But then my hunger becomes noticeable again. For the next minute, the various ideas and desires come and go. Eventually, the appetite for the biscuit is stronger than my aversion to it and so I eat the biscuit. It should be noted that this whole process, for Hobbes, is not really controlled by one's free will; it is simply the result of a mechanical process of various desires fighting against each other in my mind. In the end, one of the desires becomes the strongest and leads to an action. 'Appetites and aversions, hopes and fears, concerning one and the same thing', Hobbes says, 'arise alternately and diverse good and evil consequences of the doing, or omitting the thing propounded, come successively into view' (L 6.127). What arises and what does not arise, in other words, is not controlled by the mind, it simply happens: one does not choose, for example, to become hungry. While many philosophers would say that deliberation is carried out through free will, Hobbes disagrees. According to Hobbes, the will is simply the 'last appetite, or aversion, immediately adhering to the action or to the omission thereof' (L 6.127). So, the will itself is nothing but the final appetite or aversion just prior to the performance of the act. The will, to put it another way, does not decide which appetite or aversion to act upon, but is itself an appetite or aversion caused by factors beyond conscious control.

Hobbes's mechanistic description of human action goes hand-in-hand with a theory known as 'psychological egoism'. According to this theory, all human actions are motivated by a selfish desire to promote one's own personal benefit, one's own 'good'. The theory denies the possibility of altruism, that selfless acts are possible. The psychological egoist explains away any appearance of altruism in human action by reference to underlying selfish desires. For example, Mother Teresa's acts of kindness towards others, according to the psychological egoist, were ultimately motivated by her own desire to be loved, or to gain praise, or something of the sort. Hobbes seems to accept psychological egoism when he claims that all humans necessarily desire their own good, especially the good of self-preservation: 'For every man is desirous of what is good for him and shuns what is evil, but chiefly the chiefest of natural evils, which is death' (*Ci* 1.115). Whether Hobbes's acceptance of psychological egoism is genuine will be discussed in the Interpretation section of the present chapter. The concept of the 'good' will be further treated in the next chapter.

Hobbes's view of human nature is further developed in his treatment of 'power'. According to Hobbes, power is the means a person uses to promote his or her own good. Since we naturally desire the 'good', it follows that we also desire power. 'I put for a general inclination of all mankind', Hobbes says, 'a perpetual and restless desire of power after power that ceases only in death' (*L* 11.161). The influence of Hobbes's mechanical view of nature is clearly seen in his concept of power. The appetite for power, like all kinds of motion in the universe, stays in motion. In fact, this appetite increases in the same way that the inertial movement of falling bodies increases: 'For the nature of power is, in this point, like to fame, increasing as it proceeds; or like the motion of heavy bodies, which the further they go, make still the more haste' (*L* 10.150). In relation to human life, then, the human desire for power is not only natural, but increases as individuals achieve more power. With more power, individuals have the increased ability to satisfy their own appetites and thereby increase the 'good' that comes to them.

Compatibilism

Although Hobbes denies the existence of free will, he still carves out a space for human freedom in a determined world. Hobbes adheres to a philosophical theory known as 'compatibilism'. Compatibilists attempt to find a middle ground between the two extremes in the free will debate. On one side of this debate are *libertarian* philosophers who claim the possession of free will allows humans to choose one course of action over another. Of course, there are limits to our freedom because our will is sometimes trammelled by uncontrollable factors. Yet, for the libertarian, the future is open because not all choices are forced. Determinists, on the other hand, claim that all actions are ultimately determined by causes beyond an individual's control; freedom, for the determinist, is a comforting illusion. So, for example, assume that I am considering whether I should accept a new job offer. As I deliberate over this decision, I consider many of the possible positive and negative consequences. According to the libertarian, when I make a final decision, I am not determined to choose either one option or the other. Instead, the choice is made by an act of will that occurs outside the realm of necessary causality. On the other hand, the determinist would say that my decision, whatever it turns out to be, could not have been otherwise. I was determined, by factors outside my immediate control, to make the specific choice I made. My will, in other words, was determined to choose a specific action. Compatibilists, such as Hobbes, claim that many human actions are simultaneously free and determined. This may appear to be a puzzling claim but further reflection suggests it is not that puzzling. According to Hobbes, liberty or freedom is nothing but the 'absence of external impediments' (*L* 14.189). In other words, if a person is not physically constrained by an external force, such as chains or a prison cell, then that person is at liberty to do as he or she wills. The will of such as person, however, is subject to *necessity* because the will is simply an appetite caused by a series of motions not in the person's conscious control. Humans, therefore, can be both free and determined at the same time. In the words of Hobbes:

> *Liberty* and *necessity* are consistent. As in the water that has not only liberty, but a necessity of descending by the channel, so likewise in the actions which men voluntarily do, which (because they proceed from their will) proceed from liberty; and yet, because every act of man's will and every desire and inclination proceeds from some cause, and that from another cause, which causes in a continual chain (whose first link in the hand of God the first of all causes) proceed from *necessity* (*L* 21.263).

Interestingly, Hobbes's notions of liberty and determinism are applicable not only to humans, but also to non-living objects. As in the example above, water has the *liberty* of flowing down a channel even though it does so out of *necessity*. As we shall see in Chapter 4, Hobbes's compatibilism has perplexing moral implications.

The Nature of the Mind

When it comes to the nature of the human mind, Hobbes claims that it belongs to the same realm of reality as material bodies. Hobbes's view of the mind is part and parcel of a philosophical position known as *metaphysical monism*, according to which reality contains only one kind of substance. As we have seen, Hobbes is a materialist, so the only kind of existing substances are material bodies. In his opinion, the mind is 'reducible' to a corporeal process of internal motions. The 'mind', Hobbes says, is 'nothing more than motion occurring in various parts of an organic body.'[5] Monism may be contrasted with *metaphysical dualism*, according to which reality is divided into two kinds of substances. Descartes, who was a strong defender of dualism, believed reality to consist of both physical and mental substances. According to Descartes, the mind is metaphysically distinct from the body; the mind is an immaterial substance and the body is a material one. Although dualists believe the two substances constitute distinct realms of reality, they usually claim the mind and body interact with each other. In the Enquiry section of the current chapter, we will investigate these matters further by examining a debate between Hobbes and Descartes.

II. INTERPRETATION: IS HOBBES A PSYCHOLOGICAL OR TAUTOLOGICAL EGOIST?

In this section, we will question whether Hobbes adheres to *psychological egoism* or *tautological egoism*. According to *psychological egoism*, each individual is ultimately motivated by the selfish desire to promote his or her own good. The psychological egoist claims that altruistic acts, selflessly motivated, are impossible. Some, however, might assert that Hobbes adheres to *tautological egoism*. The tautological egoist makes the logically true claim that people desire the object of their desire. In this case, an individual's desire may be to do good for another at one's own personal expense; thus, altruistic acts are possible for the tautological egoist. A close inspection of Hobbes's text reveals evidence for conflicting interpretations of his egoism. Is he a psychological or a tautological egoist? Or is there a third option?[6]

Psychological Egoism

Psychological egoism makes the strong claim that *all* voluntary actions of *all* humans are ultimately motivated by a desire for personal gain. Put in negative terms, the psychological egoist says it is not possible to act altruistically, i.e., to act solely for the sake of another. This extreme position attempts to find a selfish motive at the root of every voluntary action. If, for example, I dedicate my life to helping the poor, the psychological egoist claims that I must gain some personal benefit from this, e.g., the praise others might lavish on me. Furthermore, that personal benefit is the primary motivating factor, according to the psychological egoist. Initially, psychological egoism seems to be a persuasive theory, especially if one believes so-called 'unselfish' acts may bring a feeling of pleasure to the one performing the act. It could be reasonably claimed that Mother Teresa was primarily motivated by the personal pleasure she received from helping the poor and needy. However, in cases where an individual gives up his or her own life for another or where an individual is not gaining pleasure in selfless acts, it is much harder to accept psychological egoism. It is difficult to discern, for example, the personal gain for an individual who covers up a live hand grenade with his or her body to save the lives of others. Of course, the psychological egoist could respond that such a hero is attempting to avoid the guilt from not acting. Whether such a response is reasonable, I will leave for you to consider. In any event, the issue here is not whether psychological egoism is a convincing philosophical position, but whether Hobbes should be considered a psychological egoist.

There are a number of passages strongly suggesting that Hobbes adheres to psychological egoism. In *De Homine*, for example, Hobbes claims that 'nature is so arranged that all desire good for themselves'.[7] Although this passage suggests psychological egoism, it does not constitute the strongest evidence because it still allows for the possibility that humans could act against their nature. Hobbes, however, seems to rule this possibility out in *De Cive* when he says that 'all men, by necessity of nature, choose that which to them appears to be less evil' (*Ci* 6.176). This point is even more clearly stated and elaborated upon in the *Elements of Law*:

> And forasmuch as necessity of nature makes men to will and desire *bonum sibi*, that which is good for themselves, and to avoid that which is

hurtful; but most of all that terrible enemy of nature, death, from whom we expect both the loss of all power, and also the greatest of bodily pains in the losing (*El* I.14.6).

On the basis of such passages, it seems reasonable to conclude that Hobbes accepts psychological egoism.

Tautological Egoism

'Tautological egoism' refers to an egoist position based on the 'tautology' that individuals desire to achieve the object of desire. A 'tautology' is a logically true proposition, which, despite being true, actually reveals nothing about the world. For example, 'if it is raining, then it is raining' or 'all human beings are human beings' are tautologies. Although both of these statements are true, they do not tell us whether it is actually raining or whether there are human beings, respectively. In reference to Hobbes, it could be argued that his definition of the 'good' as the 'object of human desire' reduces his egoism to a tautological view. According to this interpretation, Hobbes's chain of reasoning makes the following steps:

> *Premise 1.* All individuals desire their own 'good'.
> *Premise 2.* Their own good is the 'object of their desire'.
> *Conclusion.* Thus, all individuals desire the object of their desire.

If this represents Hobbes's argument, then he adheres to tautological egoism. The statement in the conclusion is a tautology that tells us no more than that the object of desire is an object of desire. This is important because tautological egoism does not rule out altruistic actions. If, for example, I desire to sacrifice my own interests for those of another, this sacrifice would still be considered my 'good' because it is what I desire. In addition, the tautological egoist position is indisputable as a philosophical view (although it may be objectionable as an interpretation of Hobbes) because to deny it would be to contradict oneself. One cannot reasonably assert, in other words, that the object of one's desire is not the object of one's desire.

The primary reason to ascribe tautological egoism to Hobbes is to strengthen his political philosophy by replacing a disputable view (psychological egoism) with an indisputable view (tautological egoism). Hobbes's political philosophy, which will be discussed more fully in Chapter 5, supposedly relies upon an egoist view of human nature. If this is the case, then it relies upon a view that many people would consider to be false or highly questionable. According to adherents of the tautological egoist interpretation of Hobbes, his political argument does not require the extreme, and probably false, position of psychological egoism. Instead, the validity of Hobbes's political argument requires only tautological egoism. To determine whether this is true, we will have to wait until we inspect his political argument. For now, we can ask whether Hobbes's texts warrant this interpretation. Some passages in Hobbes do provide support for the tautological egoist interpretation or, at the very least, do not rule it out. In *Leviathan*, for example, Hobbes offers the following definition of the good: 'But whatsoever is the object of any man's appetite or desire, that is it, which he for his part calls good' (*L* 6.120). There is nothing in this definition that requires that the good includes any kind of personal benefit to the individual concerned. A few pages later, Hobbes provides stronger support for this interpretation when he defines 'benevolence' as the 'desire of good to another' (*L* 6.123). This definition suggests that humans can desire the good of another.

Primary Passages to Consider

Is Hobbes a psychological or a tautological egoist? In this section, I present and comment upon important primary passages to help you make your own interpretative decision. After inspecting some of the textual evidence, you may make a decision on your own. You may, however, decide to postpone your final decision on this matter until you have become acquainted with Hobbes's moral and political philosophy. While direct evidence is important for arriving at an interpretation of a philosopher's position, it is also important for you to consider the broader context. What role does Hobbes's view of human nature play in his moral and political philosophy? Is psychological egoism a necessary component in his philosophical system? As you read future chapters, you may want to consider these questions. For now, a careful inspection of specific passages is an appropriate place to begin.

Comments and Questions for Passage 1

In the following passage from *Leviathan*, Hobbes elaborates upon the concept of power, which he earlier defined as the 'means to obtain some future apparent good' (*L* 10.150). If *all* people desire their own good, then it would seem to follow that *all* people should desire the means to their own good, i.e., power. In this passage, however, Hobbes claims people have a 'general inclination' to achieve power. Does this passage pose a problem for the psychological egoist interpretation of Hobbes? (Remember: the psychological egoist makes the universal claim that *all* voluntary actions of *all* humans are motivated by the desire for personal gain.)

Passage 1
So that in the first place, I put for a general inclination of all mankind, a perpetual and restless desire of power after power, that ceases only in death. And the cause of this, is not always that a man hopes for a more intensive delight than he has already attained or that he cannot be content with more moderate power, but because he cannot assure the power and means to live well, which he has at present, without the acquisition of more (*L* 11.161).

Comments and Questions for Passage 2

The psychological egoist claims that personal gain is the object of all voluntary actions. In Hobbes's case, the most important good is self-preservation. In some cases, Hobbes admits, individuals may desire death. Is the position expressed in Passage 2 consistent with the psychological egoist interpretation of Hobbes? Also, the tautological egoist claims that the good is simply the object of an individual's desire. Does the following passage call that into question? Could you reasonably argue that the following passage does not rule out altruistic actions?

Passage 2
Moreover, the greatest of goods for each is his own preservation. For nature is so arranged that all desire good for themselves. Insofar as it is within their capacities, it is necessary to desire life, health, and further, insofar as it can be done, security of future time. On the other hand, though death is the greatest of all evils (especially when accompanied by torture), the pains of life can be so great that, unless their quick end is foreseen, they may lead men to number death among the goods.[8]

Comments and Questions for Passage 3

As we saw in Chapter 2, Hobbes claims a genuine demonstrable science must begin with universal and true premises. If his science of politics is to attain the status of a genuine science, then, it must begin with a universal and true claim. In the following passage, Hobbes presents a clear statement of the foundational principle of his political philosophy. Which interpretation of Hobbes's egoism fits this passage better and why?

Passage 3

I set down for a principle, by experience known to all men and denied by none, to wit, that the dispositions of men are naturally such, that except they be restrained through fear of some coercive power, every man will distrust and dread each other; and as by natural right he may, so by necessity he will be forced to make use of the strength he has, toward the preservation of himself (*Ci* Preface. 99).

Comments and Questions for Passage 4

The tautological egoist, as we have seen, claims that altruistic actions are possible. If, for example, I gain pleasure by sacrificing my own interests for your interests, then the object of my desire is self-sacrifice; the pleasure I gain is not the motivating factor. Is the following passage, which offers a glimpse into Hobbes's view of the origin of society, consistent with the tautological egoist interpretation?

Passage 4

For when we voluntarily contract society, we look after the object of the will, that is, that which every one of those who gather together propounds to himself for good. Now whatsoever seems good is pleasant and relates either to the mind or the senses. But all the mind's pleasure is either gain or glory (or to have a good opinion of one's self) or refers to glory in the end; the rest are sensual or conducing to sensuality, which may be all comprehended under the word 'conveniences'. All society, therefore, is either for gain or for glory; that is, not so much for the love of our fellows, as for the love of ourselves (*Ci* 1.112–3).

III. ENQUIRY: WHAT IS THE NATURE OF THE MIND?

Philosophical reflection on the nature of the mind raises a number of interesting questions: What exactly is the mind? How do the mind and body interact with each other? How is the mind related to the human soul? As we have seen, Hobbes believes the mind is reducible to physical motions occurring in the brain. In his words, the mind is 'nothing more than motion occurring in various parts of an organic body'.[9] Hobbes's position is called into question by Descartes in his influential work *The Meditations on First Philosophy*. Descartes claims that his *Meditations* philosophically demonstrates the immortality of the human soul and, in consequence, its ability to exist independently of the material world. (It should be noted that Descartes, along with his contemporaries, used 'soul' and 'mind' interchangeably.) One of Descartes' associates, Marin Mersenne, sent the *Meditations* to various philosophers, including Hobbes, and requested their comments and criticisms. Fortunately for us, we now have a record of a heated philosophical exchange between Descartes and Hobbes on this topic, among others. In this section, I summarize the debate between Descartes and Hobbes on the nature of the mind and body relationship. This summary is primarily meant to provide a catalyst for your own philosophical enquiry into the nature of the human mind.

Descartes' Argument for Dualism

Descartes begins his *Meditations* by searching for a fundamental truth that can be used as a starting point for his quest for philosophical knowledge. Similarly to Hobbes, Descartes believes that any scientific demonstration must have a true and certain foundation. To find such a foundation, Descartes doubts any belief that does not meet the standard of absolute certainty. Because he realizes his senses have sometimes deceived him, Descartes considers the senses to be untrustworthy. From this realization, he concludes that any beliefs gained through sense experience cannot reach the level of absolute certainty. Descartes deepens his distrust of experience when he claims there are no definite ways to distinguish between being awake and being asleep. This leads him to the conclusion that his experiences might not accurately reveal reality. The 'facts' that apples are red, the sun is in the sky or that humans have bodies, for example, might not be true because all of these facts could simply be part of an elaborate dream. Although faced with the possibility that he may be perpetually dreaming, Descartes finds it difficult to doubt such truths as those found in mathematics and geometry. Even if he is constantly dreaming, Descartes asks, is it not true that 2×2 still equals 4? To find a reason to doubt such truths, Descartes suggests the possibility of a 'malicious demon of the utmost power and cunning' whose sole purpose is to deceive Descartes. If there were such a deceiving demon, Descartes concludes, the mathematical and geometric truths he holds to be true could actually be false. Of course, Descartes does not genuinely believe such an evil deceiver really exists, but its mere possibility suggests that nothing can be known with absolute certainty. It is at this point in his meditations that Descartes famously discovers an absolute certainty, namely, that he exists.

> Does it now follow that I too do not exist? No: if I convinced myself of something then I certainly existed. But there is a deceiver of supreme power and cunning who is deliberately and constantly deceiving me. In that case I too undoubtedly exist, if he is deceiving me; and let him deceive me as much as he can, he will never bring it about that I am nothing so long as I think I am something.[10]

Although he can doubt the existence of everything else, Descartes realizes it is impossible to doubt his own existence – even if there is an evil demon constantly deceiving him.

Descartes' indubitable truth, then, is that he exists. But what is 'he'? In the past, he considered himself to be a physical body. Yet, because knowledge of his body comes through the senses or because there may be an evil deceiver, he is not certain that his body even exists. On the other hand, he is certain that he exists. Therefore, he concludes, he must be distinct from his body.

> Hence the fact that I can clearly and distinctly understand one thing apart from another is enough to make me certain that these two things are distinct, since they are capable of being separated . . . Thus, simply by knowing that I exist and seeing at the same time that absolutely nothing else belongs to my nature or essence except that I am a thinking thing, I can infer correctly that my essence consists solely in the fact that I am a thinking thing. It is true that I may have (or, to anticipate, that I

certainly have) a body that is very closely joined to me. But nevertheless, on the one hand I have a clear and distinct idea of myself, insofar as I am simply a thinking, non-extended thing; and on the other hand I have a distinct idea of body, in so far as this is simply an extended, non-thinking thing. And accordingly, it is certain that I am really distinct from my body, and can exist without it.[11]

Descartes' true 'essence' is his mind, which is connected to his body. In fact, Descartes strengthens this connection when he says the mind is 'intermingled' with the body; the mind and the body form one 'unit'. Despite the fact that the mind and body are united, Descartes claims that they are metaphysically distinct.

Hobbes's Response to Descartes' Argument

After reading the *Meditations*, Hobbes responded with a number of objections (16 to be exact) to Descartes' arguments. For the present, we will focus on the second objection, which is concerned with the nature of the human mind. As we have seen, Descartes argues that it is impossible for him to doubt his own existence; from the fact that one is thinking, he says, it may be inferred that one exists. Hobbes accepts this initial inference as valid. From 'the fact that I am a thinking thing it follows that I exist', Hobbes says, 'since that which thinks is not nothing'.[12] Hobbes, however, raises an objection to Descartes' further inference that he is a 'mind'.

> But when the author adds, 'that is, I am a mind, or intelligence, or intellect, or reason,' a doubt arises. It does not seem to be a valid argument to say 'I am thinking, therefore I am thought' or 'I am using my intellect, hence I am an intellect.' I might just as well say 'I am walking therefore I am a walk.'[13]

What Descartes is doing, Hobbes says, is 'identifying the thing which understands with the intellect'.[14] In other words, Descartes is invalidly attributing qualities of the activity to the entity performing the activity. From the fact that the mind has thoughts, for example, one cannot infer that the mind is a thought or of the same reality as thoughts.

In contrast to Descartes, Hobbes argues that the mind actually depends upon the existence of a material subject.

It is quite certain that the knowledge of the proposition 'I exist' depends on the proposition 'I am thinking' as the author himself has explained to us. But how do we know the proposition 'I am thinking'? It can only be from our inability to conceive an act without a subject [i.e. someone performing the act]. We cannot conceive of jumping without a jumper, of knowing without a knower, or of thinking without a thinker. It seems to follow from this that a thinking thing is somehow corporeal.[15]

Hobbes argues that it is impossible for us to imagine an action without a performer. If there is a thing that is thinking, Hobbes asks, does it not follow that this 'thing' is a corporeal thing?

Mind: Material or Non-Material

You may begin your own enquiry into the nature of the human mind by evaluating the competing arguments of Descartes and Hobbes. Whose argument, in your opinion, is stronger? Whether you agree with one philosopher or the other, there are difficulties for both positions. If you agree with Descartes' view that the mind is not physical, you are faced with the difficulty of trying to explain how the mind and body interact. Although Descartes believed that the mind interacted with the body through the pineal gland, which is a small organ in the brain, he failed to provide a real answer to the question of the mind and body relationship. Simply put, how does an immaterial mind that does not exist in time or place affect or influence a physical body and vice versa? Yet, if you accept Hobbes's materialist view of the human mind, you are faced with an equally puzzling question: What does it mean to say that our mind is 'nothing but' physical motions in the brain? Does it make sense to say that a sensation of happiness is *no more* than a neuron firing in the brain? Isn't it more than that? These are just some questions to start you on a philosophical enquiry into the nature of the mind.

CONCLUSION

In this chapter, we have seen that Hobbes holds the following metaphysical beliefs: (1) reality is comprised of 'matter in motion'; (2) the motions of natural bodies, including the actions of humans, follow mechanistic laws; (3) only individual entities exist; (4) human actions, though subject to necessary laws, may still be free; (5) the mind is nothing but physical motions occurring in the mind; and (6) individuals naturally desire to promote their own good. After the summary of the main points, an interpretative conflict concerning Hobbes's view of egoism was presented. According to one interpretation, Hobbes is a psychological egoist who believes that the voluntary actions of all humans are ultimately motivated by a desire for personal gain. By contrast, it could also be argued that Hobbes is a tautological egoist who advances the logically true claim that individuals desire the object of their desire. The last section of the chapter presented a debate between Descartes and Hobbes on the nature of the human mind. Hobbes, as we saw, criticizes Descartes' belief that the mind and body are metaphysically distinct.

CHAPTER 4

HOBBES'S MORAL PHILOSOPHY

Moral philosophy raises questions about how humans ought to live their lives: What is the nature of justice? Do we have moral obligations to perform certain kinds of actions? Are moral standards absolute or relative? What is the basis for moral obligation? What does it mean to say we are obliged to do something? For Hobbes, moral and political philosophy are closely related because, as we shall see, the former has consequences for the latter. Thus, before we can really understand Hobbes's political philosophy, we must first examine his ideas about morality.[1] It must be noted, however, that Hobbes uses the phrase 'moral philosophy' to cover all of his philosophical reflections on human nature. Using today's terminology, some of Hobbes's reflections on human behaviour would be best characterized as 'psychological' rather than 'moral'. To put it another way, Hobbes uses 'moral philosophy' in a much broader sense than philosophers do today. In this chapter, we will look at Hobbes's moral philosophy, using today's understanding of this term. In the first section, I present the main elements of this philosophy. As we shall see, Hobbes appears to be a moral relativist who believes there are no natural standards of morality. Since many of his moral views are revealed in his description of the 'state of nature', a fair portion of the first section is devoted to a discussion of this state. In the second section, contrasting interpretations of Hobbes's 'state of nature' and 'laws of nature' will be presented. The main question addressed in this section is whether Hobbes's state of nature is a genuine moral wasteland devoid of natural standards of morality. The chapter concludes with an enquiry into competing ideas on the state of nature. John Locke, another English political philosopher from the seventeenth century, presented his own description of life in the state of nature, a description that differs in important ways from Hobbes's. After examining their contrasting accounts, you can decide for yourself whose is stronger.

I. SUMMARY: HOBBES'S MORAL PHILOSOPHY

Moral Relativism

Hobbes adheres to a philosophical position known as *moral relativism*. According to a moral relativist, there are no natural standards by which to assess the moral status of our actions. Natural standards of morality, if they exist, provide a set of ethical rules or guidelines that are in force at all times and in all places. For example, many people would claim that torturing innocent people for no reason would be naturally wrong at all times and in all places. *Moral realists* admit the existence of such standards. According to the moral realist, certain practices, even if they are socially accepted, might still be immoral. Slavery, for example, is always wrong, even if it is, or was, a common practice. In contrast to the moral realist, the moral relativist claims that all moral standards are relative to a particular individual or culture. Thus, moral relativism is divided into two types: individual and cultural. *Individual moral relativism* states that moral standards are relative to each individual. What is right and what is wrong is decided upon by each person. *Cultural moral relativism* states that moral standards are relative to a certain culture, society or nation.

Interestingly, Hobbes adheres to both forms of relativism. When he considers individuals in isolation, he reveals his commitment to individual moral relativism. On the other hand, when he talks about individuals as members of a community, he reveals his commitment to cultural moral relativism. As we have seen, Hobbes's method leads him to dissolve the commonwealth and look at its parts (i.e. humans) in isolation before he imaginatively recomposes the commonwealth. In the previous chapter, we saw that Hobbes's study of human nature included the view that the 'good' is simply the object of a person's desire. Given the fact that different people desire different things, it follows that the 'good' changes from person to person. The 'words of good, evil, and contemptible', Hobbes says, 'are ever used with relation to the person that uses them; there being nothing simply and absolutely so' (*L* 6.120). If I desire to enslave another person for my own purposes, for example, then the practice of slavery is 'good' to me. In other words, slavery is neither right nor wrong by nature. Hobbes's individual relativism shifts to cultural relativism when he considers individuals as members of a political community who make agreements with each other to abide by the laws. A 'common standard of virtues and vices', Hobbes says, 'does not appear except in civil life; this standard cannot, for this reason, be other than the laws of each and every state.'[2] For Hobbes, after the formation of civil states, the laws of each state define the standards of morality. If slavery is wrong in a particular state, then it is wrong relative to the citizens of that state, but not absolutely.

PERPLEXING PROBLEM: THE PROBLEM OF FREEDOM AND MORAL RESPONSIBILITY

In the previous chapter, Hobbes's compatibilist view of human action was discussed. According to this view, as long as an individual is not physically prevented from doing what is willed, then that individual is 'free'. However, Hobbes also holds the determinist view that the will itself is determined; in other words, human choices are not freely chosen. Here, I would like to show how Hobbes's compatibilism raises a perplexing problem. It is a commonly accepted truth that individuals should be held morally responsible only for those actions under their control. For example, imagine that a man drinks a soft drink that, unknown to him, contains a powerful hallucinogenic drug that was placed in the drink by his evil neighbour. Further imagine that the man, completely under the influence of the hallucinogen, begins shooting at people as they walk past his house. If this man has no reasonable expectation that his drink would contain such a drug, should he be held morally (or even legally) responsible for his actions? If you answer 'no' to this question, then you probably accept the 'principle of responsibility'. According to this principle, a person's moral responsibility is directly proportional to the level of freedom at which the person acted. The 'level of freedom' refers to how much control an individual possesses over his or her actions. In the example above, the drugged man did not freely choose to take the hallucinogenic drug. In addition, there was no reasonable expectation that the soft drink contained such a drug. Thus, in this case, the man's responsibility level is low because the level of freedom is low. Other cases show that there are various levels of freedom. For example, imagine a female military cadet who is threatened with expulsion if she publicly speaks of the sexual harassment of her commanding officer. The cadet decides to go AWOL. Is the cadet 'free' in this situation? Would you blame her morally for neglecting her duty? Or, imagine a man who carefully plans a terrorist attack and then methodically follows through with the plans. Are not these actions more free than those of the drugged man and the cadet? Each of these examples reveals different levels of freedom.

A problem arises when one simultaneously accepts the view that human actions are determined and the principle of responsibility. According to determinists, no human actions are freely chosen; instead, all actions are ultimately determined by factors, such as hereditary or environmental factors, that are beyond one's immediate control. In Hobbes's view, the physical motions occurring in the brain cause a person to act in certain ways. Nevertheless, Hobbes speaks as if people should be held morally responsible for their actions. For example, as we shall see in Chapter 6, Hobbes blames a variety of religious leaders for their participation in causing the English Civil War. In this case, he speaks as if they have done something wrong. Yet, if all human actions are not freely chosen, then why should anyone be blamed (or praised) for anything? Of course, one may point out that Hobbes is technically a compatibilist who argues that human actions are both free and determined. According to this definition of freedom, however, even a river can be 'free'. Yet, would we hold a river morally responsible for its actions? Can freedom, in Hobbes's sense, be used to justify the moral assessment of an individual's actions? How do you think Hobbes would respond to this problem?

Self-Preservation: A Natural Standard of Morality?

One may be tempted to say that Hobbes's view of self-preservation provides a natural standard of morality since everyone seems to have a natural desire to avoid death. If it were the case that *all* individuals desire the good of self-preservation, then it would seem to be a universal good not relative to individuals. For two reasons, however, Hobbes's view of self-preservation does not provide a universal moral standard. First, Hobbes does not consistently claim that everyone always believes that self-preservation is good. As we saw in the last chapter, some people may desire their own death as the better of two or more options. Thus, self-preservation is not always a good. Second, even if each and every person did desire self-preservation, this would simply tell us that people *do* avoid death, not that they *should*. Hobbes's claim that people desire self-preservation, in other words, is *descriptive* and not *prescriptive*. To say that one has a moral obligation, however, is to say that one *ought* to pursue the good, not simply that one *does* pursue the good. Moral standards *prescribe* what we ought to do, rather than *describe* what we actually do.

The State of Nature: Preliminaries

Hobbes is probably most famous for his description of life as 'solitary, poor, nasty, brutish, and short' (*L* 13.186). It must be emphasized, however, that these terms apply to life in a 'state of nature' and not to life in a commonwealth. The state of nature is a hypothetical situation in which there is no civil law, no police force, no judicial system and no overarching power to keep people in check. It is not an historical account of life prior to the formation of government; rather, it represents any situation where individuals are free from civil laws and their corresponding punishments. Individuals shipwrecked on a deserted island, for example, could be said to exist in a state of nature. If rules and penalties were established, however, they would no longer be in such a state.

Hobbes's state of nature is often interpreted as a consequence of the application of his philosophical method to political and moral matters.[3] In the first chapter, we saw that Hobbes uses a resolutive-compositive method to understand bodies scientifically. In accordance with this method, a philosophical study of a particular body begins with a resolution into its primary components. The next step is to study the individual parts in isolation. Hobbes then tries to uncover how the parts come together to form the whole. In his moral (and political) philosophy, the steps of this methodology are easy to discern. First, Hobbes resolves the political body into its 'parts' (i.e. humans) and further resolves humans into their 'parts' (i.e. appetites, aversions and other 'internal motions'). After the resolution is complete, Hobbes begins his composition of the commonwealth by explaining the behaviour of isolated individuals. The individuals are then joined together into the apolitical state of nature in order to study how and why they unite to form a political body. Hobbes's depiction of the state of nature not only grounds his political philosophy, but clearly indicates his moral views because it describes the moral standards, if any, that exist in a 'natural condition of mankind'.

One of the most pressing questions in moral philosophy is whether there are any moral standards that apply to all individuals, societies and nations. The concept of the state of nature, when used as a philosophical thought experiment, provides an excellent model for theorizing about natural moral standards. Although Hobbes presents slightly different versions of the state of nature in his various works on political philosophy, the central ideas remain basically the same. Here, the summary of Hobbes's state of nature is based on *Leviathan*. An interesting project for your own interpretation would be to compare and contrast the various accounts given in the *Elements of Law*, *De Cive* and *Leviathan*.

Morality in the State of Nature

Hobbes's state of nature is basically a moral wasteland where anything goes. In this state, Hobbes says, 'nothing can be unjust' since the 'notions of right and wrong, justice and injustice have there no place' (*L* 13.188). In other words, there are no natural standards for judging the morality or immorality of actions. The state of nature is a moral vacuum, according to Hobbes, primarily because it is a state of war 'where every man is enemy to every man' (*L* 13.186). The state of nature is conflict-ridden for three reasons. First, Hobbes claims that individuals in the state of nature are equal; this equality, combined with the lack of a given resource, leads to a competitive situation where individuals become enemies. By 'equal', Hobbes does not mean they are exactly alike in mind or in body. Instead, 'equality' refers to the ability each person possesses to kill others. Despite the fact that some people are 'manifestly stronger in body' or 'of quicker mind', Hobbes says, 'when all is reckoned together, the difference between man and man is not so considerable', and the 'weakest has strength to kill the strongest' (*L* 13.183). A scrawny weakling, for example, could kill a muscular athlete while the latter lay sleeping. According to Hobbes, such equality leads to conflict when individuals simultaneously desire a scarce resource that cannot be held in common. From the 'equality of ability', Hobbes says, there 'arises an equality of hope in the attaining of our ends' such that, if two people desire the same thing, they will 'become enemies' (*L* 13.184). In such a situation, everyone attempts to 'destroy or subdue' others in order to attain the desired commodity (*L* 13.184). This leads to a general state of distrust, or what Hobbes calls 'diffidence', in the state of nature. Because of this distrust, which Hobbes names as the second cause of conflict, some people will try to defend themselves by the use of preemptive attacks on their enemies. One may strike first to prevent enemies from future strikes on oneself. These two causes of conflict, competition and diffidence are joined by a third: the natural desire for glory. Humans naturally desire to be esteemed by others and when such esteem is not given, they are inclined to demand it through force. According to Hobbes, then, conflicts in the state of nature ultimately lead to an all-out war of everyone against everyone.

Moral Terminology and the State of Nature

In his description of life in the state of nature, Hobbes uses a number of terms that usually carry moral connotations. Upon further inspection, however, it is easy to recognize that his use of such terms does not imply the existence of natural moral standards. Take, for example, the term 'equality'. People often claim that the equality of humans provides a basis for a claim to moral rights. Because we are created equal, it is often argued, we have the natural right to such things as life, liberty and the pursuit of happiness. Although Hobbes says individuals are equal in the state of nature, his notion of equality carries no moral force; it simply describes an actual human ability, namely, the ability to kill. Hobbes also claims that individuals in a state of nature possess a 'natural right' or 'right of nature'. According to the common definition of this term, individuals possess a certain set of moral rights. It could be argued, for example, that individuals shipwrecked on a deserted island possess the 'natural right' not to be harmed without cause. An infringement of this natural right would be *wrong*. By contrast, Hobbes defines natural right as the liberty to perform any action necessary to self-preservation. According to this definition, individuals in a state of nature *decide for themselves* what is or is not required for their own preservation. In other words, there are no objective rules or guidelines to determine what is necessary to stay alive, So there are no moral constraints on human behaviour. The term 'liberty' usually has moral connotations, as do the terms 'equality' and 'natural right'. In Hobbes's philosophy, however, it is hard to see how it has anything to do with morality. As we saw in Chapter 3, Hobbes defines 'liberty' as the absence of external constraints. To say I am 'free' or 'at liberty' means no more than to say I am not physically constrained. In this sense, even a river can be 'free'. Although individuals in the state of nature are *free*, *equal* and possess *natural rights*, then, one could argue that they do not possess any *moral* rights in this state.

The Laws of Nature

Although Hobbes says the concepts of 'right' and 'wrong' have no role in the state of nature, he also says that there are 'laws of nature' that forbid or command certain kinds of actions. The fact that these laws apply to human behaviour in the state of nature could be used to support the interpretation that Hobbes actually accepts the existence of natural moral standards. Scholars disagree over whether the laws of nature should be interpreted as moral laws. This disagreement will be investigated in the Interpretation section of this chapter. Here, a summary of the laws of nature will be presented. Hobbes's 'laws of nature' are central not only to his moral philosophy, but also to his political philosophy. The following summary focuses on the morally relevant features.

As mentioned in the first chapter, Hobbes's notion of scientific demonstration is modelled on the science of geometry. In this science, basic principles are laid down and conclusions are deduced from them. The influence of geometry is clearly seen in Hobbes's deduction of the laws of nature. Hobbes begins by defining his terms and then draws conclusions according to logical rules. A law of nature, Hobbes says, is a rule discovered by rational reflection that leads individuals towards self-preservation. Through the power of reason, in other words, individuals in the state of nature can discover general principles of action that will help them avoid destruction. The first law of nature, according to Hobbes, is that every person should strive to establish a state of peace whenever possible, but continue to fight if others do not cooperate. The first law of nature has two parts to it, what Hobbes refers to as the 'fundamental law of nature' and the 'sum of the right of nature'. The first part is called the 'fundamental law of nature' because it guides one towards the fulfilment of his or her fundamental natural desire, the desire to preserve oneself. Of course, in many cases, a peacemaker is often susceptible to harm by those who will take advantage of him or her. If only one person seeks peace and others do not cooperate, then it is more rational for the peacemaker to abandon the attempt and to fight to stay alive. Thus, there is a need for the second part of the first law of nature, i.e., the 'sum of the right of nature'. The 'right of nature', as we have already seen, is the liberty to do whatever is necessary for self-preservation. In situations where peace is unlikely or impossible, Hobbes says, each person rationally discovers that survival requires the 'helps of war'. In such situations, one must rely on the natural right to protect oneself, even if it means remaining in a state of war.

Other laws of nature logically follow, in Hobbes's opinion, from the first law. Hobbes believes that the retention of natural rights is responsible for the warlike conditions of the state of nature. For example, if I lived in a state of nature, I would have the natural right to imprison, enslave or kill others if such actions promoted my own self-preservation. As long as I exercised this right, then, I would continue to promote war. The first law of nature, however, states that I must seek peace. It logically follows that I must 'lay down' my natural right if a state of peace is to be created.

According to Hobbes, individuals 'lay down' the right of nature in one of two ways: by transferring or renouncing. To *transfer* a right is to grant it to another specific individual. To *renounce* a right is simply to give up your right without giving it to anyone in particular. To establish a state of peace and thereby escape from the state of nature, Hobbes says, individuals must collectively *transfer* their natural rights to an individual, or to a group of individuals, who will then use their newly granted authority to create laws and a system to enforce those laws. To put it simply, to escape from the state of nature, individuals form a covenant with each other to create a political body that has the power and authority to govern them. (The political aspects of the covenant will be covered in the next chapter.)

The third law of nature, Hobbes says, requires that 'men perform their covenants made' (*L* 15.201). According to Hobbes, a covenant is a kind of contract wherein one or both parties in a particular agreement agree to the performance of some action at a later date. For example, if I give you money to paint my house tomorrow, and you agree, we have made a *covenant*. If, however, I give you money for your car and you immediately transfer ownership, then we have made a simple *contract*. With regard to the political covenant, individuals make an agreement with each other to abide by the future decisions of the sovereign power. The third law of nature, then, naturally follows from the preceding one because people must stick to their agreements if the newly created government is to be effective. According to Hobbes, the third law of nature is the 'fountain and original [i.e. origin] of justice', (*L* 15.202). The concepts of justice and injustice, as we have already seen, are not present in the state of nature. Once individuals agree to create a common power, however, certain types of actions can legitimately be considered just or unjust. More specifically, justice is the practice of abiding by one's covenants, or, to be more precise, valid covenants. Injustice is the breaking of one's valid covenants. There are a number of conditions that can invalidate covenants, such as the reasonable suspicion that another party in an agreement intends to back out. In certain cases, then, individuals would be able justly to disregard the covenant. These will be discussed in Chapter 5. For present purposes, it is important to note that the third law of nature converts a moral wasteland 'where nothing can be just or unjust' into a state where moral concepts apply. For example, in the state of nature individuals may justly steal goods from others since there are no rules forbidding individuals from doing so. Once civil laws prohibiting stealing are established, however, stealing becomes unjust. To what extent the third law of nature, and the others, create a genuine moral system will be considered in the Interpretation section.

Hobbes deduces 16 more laws of nature that all promote peace among the citizens in a commonwealth. The fourth law of nature, for example, claims that the expression of gratitude for benefits freely received from others helps promote peace among individuals. As another example, the eleventh law of nature demands that any individual serving as a judge in a dispute must treat the disputants equally. The twelfth law of nature commands that people enjoy things in common that cannot be divided. At the end of his deduction of the laws of nature, Hobbes says 'these are the laws of nature dictating peace for a means of conservation of men in multitudes' (*L* 15.214). He states that there are other laws of nature forbidding such things as drunkenness, yet these laws are not worthy of being mentioned because they threaten individuals and not the community. In addition, Hobbes claims that all the laws of nature may be

summarized quite simply in the golden rule, 'Do not that to another which thou would not have done to oneself' (*L* 15.214).

PERPLEXING PROBLEM: THE PROBLEM OF REASON IN THE STATE OF NATURE

The state of nature, Hobbes says, is a state of war of all against all primarily because each individual retains a natural right to do whatever they believe is necessary to preserve themselves. In warlike conditions, then, it seems quite *reasonable* to protect yourself by not trusting others. On the other hand, Hobbes says that the laws of nature, which are 'dictates of *reason*', are supposed to lead to a state of peace. It appears, then, that reason, when exercised in a state of nature, simultaneously points towards war and peace. So how can reason lead us out of a state of nature when it also suggests that we stay in a state of war? How might Hobbes reply to this question?

link to the moral *Obligation* of
underguments Hobbes

The third law of nature is the source of 'obligation'. People put themselves under an obligation, Hobbes says, when they transfer or renounce a certain right. If I completely renounce my natural right to fish in the river, for example, then I oblige myself 'not to hinder' others from fishing in the river. What exactly does this mean? What kind of obligation is Hobbes talking about? Before attempting to answer these questions, we should recognize some important points about the concept of 'obligation'. In the first case, statements expressing obligations are usually 'ought' statements. If I am obliged to tell you the truth, then I 'ought' to tell you the truth. Second, the word 'ought' may be used in different contexts. For example, my doctor may inform me that I 'ought' to take a certain drug if I wish to stop sneezing from seasonal allergies. Philosophers refer to this kind of 'ought' statement as a *hypothetical* or *prudential* imperative (or command). The doctor's statement is a command telling me that *if* I have the goal of ending the allergic reaction, *then* I 'ought' to take a certain drug. In this sense, the 'ought' does not necessarily count as an 'obligation' in any meaningful sense of the word. Although I 'ought' to take my medicine, in other words, it is not the case that I am 'obliged' to do so. We usually use 'obligation' in either a legal or moral sense. As a citizen of a particular society, I have certain legal obligations. I have a legal obligation, for example, to register my automobile with the proper authorities. Thus, in a legal sense, one might say that I 'ought' to register my car. If I fail to do so, I am acting illegally, but not immorally. In addition, it seems that we have moral obligations to perform or avoid certain kinds of actions. If I were a man with a wife and three children and I am stricken with an easily curable disease, most people would say that I am morally obliged, or that I 'ought', to fight the disease and stay alive. In the case of moral and legal obligations, we 'ought' to do something because there is a law that commands us to do it. What we might call the 'moral point of view' is that there are moral laws which we ought to obey simply because following such laws is the right thing to do. When Hobbes speaks of obligation, then, does he mean moral or legal obligations? Or, does 'obligation' refer to a hypothetical imperative? These and other questions will be pursued in the Interpretation section, where the moral status of Hobbes's law of nature is questioned.

PERPLEXING PROBLEM: THE PROBLEM OF THE FOOL

In his treatment of the third law of nature that demands that people fulfil their covenants, Hobbes raises the hypothetical objection of the 'fool'. The 'fool has said in his heart', Hobbes says, 'that there is no such thing as justice' (L 15.203). In addition, the fool further claims that there is no reason to perform one's covenants if such performance is contrary to one's own interests and if one can break the covenant without being caught. Imagine, for example, that I am in a busy market without money and that I am very hungry. Now, as a citizen of a commonwealth, I have covenanted to abide by the civil laws, one of which prohibits stealing. Assuming that I could steal an apple without being detected and thereby satisfy my hunger, would it not be reasonable for me to do so? Assume further that there is no God, or other divine being, that could or would punish me for this theft because, as Hobbes points out, the fool also does not believe in God. According to the fool, reason would direct a person in this situation to steal the apple because 'all the voluntary actions of men tend to the benefit of themselves' and 'those actions are most reasonable that conduce most to their ends' (L 15.204). Hobbes offers two responses that show why the fool is foolish. First, there is always the possibility that a covenant-breaker might get caught. Even if the chance of one's crime being discovered is slim, Hobbes believes it is still contrary to reason to take that chance. Second, Hobbes points out that individuals in the state of nature must rely on others for self-defence. By breaking covenants, one is running the risk of being cast out of society and into a state of nature, where individuals must fend for themselves. Is Hobbes's response to the fool a good one?

II. INTERPRETATION: ARE HOBBES'S LAWS OF NATURE PRUDENTIAL PRECEPTS OR MORAL OBLIGATIONS?

In this section, we will investigate whether Hobbes's state of nature is a genuine moral wasteland, completely void of natural standards of right or wrong. Two conflicting interpretations of Hobbes's laws of nature will be presented: the *prudential interpretation* and the *moral interpretation*. The prudential interpretation claims that the laws of nature are not genuine moral rules, but prudential recommendations that point out rational means for individuals to preserve themselves.[4] The moral interpretation, by contrast, says that the laws of nature, in addition to being prudential recommendations, are also moral rules that humans are obliged to follow.[5] After examining the evidence for both interpretations, you may decide for yourself which interpretation is stronger.

The Prudential Interpretation of the Laws of Nature

According to the prudential interpretation, the laws of nature *recommend* certain types of behaviour that ultimately promote self-preservation. In *Leviathan*, Hobbes defines a law of nature as a 'precept or general rule, found out by reason, by which a man is forbidden to do that which is destructive of his life or takes away the means of the same' (*L* 14.189). For adherents of the prudential interpretation, when Hobbes says a law of nature 'forbids' or 'commands' certain actions, as the case may be, this is not to be taken in a literal sense; the laws of nature do not forbid actions *simply because they are morally wrong* nor do they command certain actions *because they are morally right*. Instead, the laws of nature either forbid certain actions *because such actions threaten one's preservation* or command certain actions *because such actions promote one's self-preservation*. In other words, if you want to preserve yourself, you will follow the

prudential
authoritarian
no moral

laws of nature. According to this interpretation, Hobbes's laws of nature are not really *moral* laws. If I am motivated to do the morally correct thing simply because it is good for me, one might argue, then I am not acting with the proper motivation for the action to be recognized as being within the realm of morality. Imagine that I donate money to a charitable organization simply to impress a woman I am romantically interested in. In this case, I have no inclination or desire to do the right thing. Instead, I am acting on pure self-interest. According to many philosophers, this kind of action is neither moral nor immoral. I may be doing the right thing, but I am not doing it for the right reason. As it turns out, Hobbes's laws of nature do recommend traditionally *moral* behaviour. For example, the laws of nature, as we have seen, demand that individuals seek peace with each other whenever possible, that they stick to agreements, that they express gratitude for benefits received, and so on. These kinds of actions are traditionally considered to be 'moral'. For the prudential interpretation, however, Hobbes's laws of nature prescribe such behaviour only because it promotes one's own interests, not because the actions are moral. In other words, according to this interpretation, Hobbes believes you should behave morally because you will benefit by doing so, not because it is the right thing to do.

The prudential interpretation is supported by the fact that Hobbes claims the concepts of right and wrong do not apply in the state of nature (at least prior to the political covenant). Before the establishment of government and civil laws, no one is restricted by any moral rules at all. Although the laws of nature are in effect, the prudential interpretation says, they should not be considered genuine 'laws'. It is claimed that Hobbes once again turns a morally relevant concept into an amoral one. As we have seen, Hobbes removes the moral connotations from such terms as 'equality', 'liberty' and 'right of nature'. A law of nature, technically speaking, is not really a law at all, especially not a moral one. According to Hobbes's definition, a law of nature is a rule that commands moral behaviour not because it is moral; rather, it is a rule discovered by rational reflection that promotes the self-interests of individuals.

The Moral Interpretation of the Laws of Nature

The moral interpretation, in contrast to the prudential interpretation, asserts that Hobbes's laws of nature are not only prudential precepts, but also laws that humans are *morally obliged* to follow. Hobbes claims that the laws of nature may be viewed from two perspectives. First, the laws of nature are a series of rules discovered by human reason. In this case, the laws of nature are not morally obligatory; instead, they are prudential precepts that provide a rational path to self-preservation. Second, the laws of nature are also the commands of God revealed through the natural power of reason and through Holy Scripture. In this case, the laws of nature are morally obligatory and are properly called 'laws'. According to Hobbes, when he says that the laws of nature 'command' or 'prohibit', he is speaking loosely. Technically speaking, only someone with the proper authority commands or prohibits human actions. God, Hobbes says, does possess such authority over humans.

> The dictates of reason, men used to call by the name of laws, but improperly; for they are but conclusions or theorems concerning what conduces to the conservation and defense of themselves; whereas law, properly, is the word of him that by right has command over others. But yet if we consider the same theorems, as delivered in the word of God, who by right commands all things, then they are properly called laws (*L* 15.216–7).

In a limited sense, then, the moral interpretation accepts the basic assertion of the prudential interpretation: that the laws of nature are prudential precepts. However, the moral interpretation further asserts that the laws of nature, when considered as the word of God, oblige humans to the performance of virtuous acts. Why Hobbes believes that God has the authority to command humans will be discussed in Chapter 6, which covers his religious views.

The moral interpretation finds evidence in Hobbes's specific claim that the laws of nature are moral laws. In *De Cive*, Hobbes raises the issue of whether the natural law should be identified with the moral law. 'All writers do agree', Hobbes says, 'that the natural law is the same with the moral. Let us see whether this is true' (*Ci* 3.150). To answer this question, he recalls the important point that people have different conceptions of good and evil because of their contrasting appetites and aversions. As long as people continue to disagree about moral conceptions, Hobbes says, they will be in a state of conflict. Yet, in the state of war, everyone recognizes that war is evil and peace is good.

They are, therefore, so long in the state of war, as by reason of the diversity of the present appetites, they mete good and evil by diverse measures. All men easily acknowledge this state, as long as they are in it, to be evil and by consequence, that peace is good. They, therefore, who could not agree concerning a present [good], do agree concerning a future good, which indeed is a work of reason (*Ci* 3.150–1).

According to the moral interpretation, the notion that there is a universal good supports the idea that objective moral standards exist in the state of nature. Hobbes supposedly confirms this when he claims that the natural law demands moral behaviour and should therefore be identified with the moral law.

Reason declaring peace to be good, it follows that the means to peace be good also; and therefore that modesty, equity, trust, humanity, mercy (which we have demonstrated to be necessary to peace), are good manners or habits, that is, virtues. The [natural] law therefore, in the means to peace, commands also good manners or the practice of virtue; and therefore, it is called *moral* (*Ci* 3.151).

As a moral law, the natural law provides a universal standard that transcends all individual and cultural notions of the good. This interpretation is further supported when Hobbes claims that the:

laws of nature are immutable and eternal; what they forbid, can never be lawful; what they command, can never be unlawful. For pride, ingratitude, breach of contracts (or injury), inhumanity, contumely, will never be lawful, nor the contrary virtues to these ever unlawful (*Ci* 3.149).

According to the moral interpretation, Hobbes is claiming that virtuous behaviour will always be *good* and vicious behaviour will always be *bad*, which confirms that Hobbes's laws of nature are moral laws.

Primary Passages to Consider
Comments and Questions on Passage 1

According to Hobbes, a law is a command that individuals are obliged to follow. Laws, however, must be issued by a law-giver or else they are not genuine laws. In Passage 1, Hobbes explains that the laws of nature are not properly laws but are just 'qualities that dispose men to peace'. Does this passage provide support for the prudential interpretation? On the other hand, Hobbes says that the laws of nature lead people towards traditional moral virtues, such as equity and gratitude. Does this not provide support for the moral interpretation? Which position, if any, does the following passage really support?

Passage 1
For the laws of nature, which consist in equity, justice, gratitude, and other moral virtues on these depending, in the condition of mere nature are not laws, but qualities that dispose me to peace and to obedience (*L* 26.314).

Comments and Questions on Passage 2

Advocates of the two interpretations under consideration disagree over whether Hobbes's use of moral terminology in his account of the state of nature is genuine. 'Obligation', as we have seen, is a term like 'law of nature' or 'equality' insofar as it usually carries moral connotations. In Passage 1, Hobbes claims that the laws of nature are always obligatory in one's conscience, even if they are not always obligatory in outward behaviour. According to the moral interpretation, this means that individuals are *morally obliged* not only to intend to perform virtuous actions, but actually to perform such actions when it is safe to do so. For example, Hobbes claims that one of the laws of nature commands that I attempt to establish a state of peace with my enemies. Yet, in many situations, my enemies, who are either driven by greed or guided by poor thinking, may not want to cooperate with me. They may, in other words, desire to stay in a state of war. In such situations, Hobbes says, I am still obliged to intend peace in my conscience, but I am not obliged to act virtuously. According to the moral interpretation, when Hobbes says we are *obliged* by the laws of nature, he means that we are *commanded* to act in some ways and *forbidden* to act in other ways. The laws of nature, in other words, do not simply *suggest* or *recommend*, but *demand*. Does the following passage imply that it would be *morally wrong* to act against the law of nature?

Passage 2
But because most men, by reason of their perverse desire of present profit, are very unapt to observe these laws, although acknowledged by

them, if perhaps some, more humble than the rest, should exercise that equity and usefulness which reason dictates, those not practicing the same, surely they would not follow reason in so doing; nor would they hereby procure themselves peace, but a more certain quick destruction and the keepers of the law become a mere prey to the breakers of it. It is not therefore to be imagined, that by nature, that is, by reason, men are obliged to the exercise of all these laws in that state of men wherein they are not practiced by others. We are obliged yet, in the interim, to a readiness of mind to observe them whenever their observation shall seem to conduce to the end for which they were ordained. We must therefore conclude that the law of nature does always and everywhere oblige in the internal court, or that of conscience, but not always in the external court, but then only when it may be done with safety (*Ci* 3.149).

Comments and Questions on Passage 3

In Passage 3, Hobbes provides a definition of obligation: one becomes 'obliged' by transferring or renouncing a right to something. If, for example, I renounce my right to the fish in the river in order to establish a state of peace with my enemies, I become 'obliged' not to interfere when they go fishing. Interestingly, Hobbes claims that the 'bonds' that oblige me to this agreement are fears of the consequences of breaking it. Thus, it would seem that the only reason for me not to break my covenant is because I might be punished for so doing. But if I am only obliged to do something because I am fearful of the consequences, am I really *morally obliged*? Does this change your interpretation of Hobbes's view of 'obligation'? Is it really a 'moral' obligation that is created by the making of covenants?

Passage 3
And when a man hath in either manner abandoned, or granted away his right, then he is said to be obliged, or bound, not to hinder those to whom such a right is granted or abandoned from the benefit of it and that he ought, and it is his duty, not to make void that voluntary act of his own . . . The way by which man either simply renounces or transfers this right is a declaration or signification, by some voluntary and sufficient sign or signs, that he does so renounce or transfer . . . And these signs are either words only or actions only, or (as it happens most often) both words and actions. And the same are the bonds, by which men are bound and obliged, that have their strength, not from their own nature

(for nothing is more easily broken then a man's word), but from fear of some evil consequence upon the rupture (*L* 14.191–92).

Comments and Questions on Passage 4

As we have seen, the moral interpretation claims that the laws of nature are genuine moral laws that humans are *morally obliged* to follow. As such, it would seem that it is morally right (or good) to adhere to the laws of nature and morally wrong (or evil) to break them. In the following passage, Hobbes explains why it is *good* to follow the laws and *evil* to break them. In this explanation, do you think the terms 'good' and 'evil' are used in a genuine moral sense?

Passage 4
Every man by natural passion, calls that good which pleases him for the present, or so far forth as he can foresee; and in like manner that which displeases him [is called] evil. And, therefore, he that foresees the whole way to his preservation (which is the end that every one by nature aims at) must also call it good and the contrary evil. And this is that good and evil, which not every man in passion calls so, but all men by reason. And therefore the fulfilling of all these laws is good in reason and the breaking of them evil (*El* I.17.14).

III. ENQUIRY: DO MORAL LAWS EXIST IN THE STATE OF NATURE?

The concept of the state of nature provides an excellent tool for investigating the nature of morality. While it is primarily used to raise political questions about the origin and legitimacy of government, it may also be used effectively to investigate moral issues. One of the most pressing questions in moral philosophy is whether there are objective moral standards that can be used to assess the moral status of actions, motives, practices or institutions. For example, most people have come to realize that slavery is a moral evil and, as a consequence, that laws allowing such a practice are unjust. To make the claim that a civil law is unjust, one must have a conception of justice that transcends particular times and places. One method for enquiring into the existence of such moral standards is to imagine a state without governing bodies, legal enforcement and judicial systems, i.e., a state of nature, and to question whether there are any natural rules or laws. As we have seen, Hobbes uses the state of nature as a method for enquiry into moral issues, among other things. Hobbes was not alone in employing the conceptual tool of the state of nature. In each major period of philosophy, one or more philosophers have employed the concept of the state of nature, or something similar, as a means of philosophical investigation. In this section, you will be introduced to John Locke's description of the state of nature. Locke was an English philosopher who was born in 1632. His philosophical interests led him into a variety of different fields of enquiry, including political philosophy. The main work of interest for the present purposes is the *Second Treatise of Government*, wherein Locke supports the doctrine of a limited government and defends the right to revolt against tyranny. In common with Hobbes, Locke uses the state of nature as a means for arguing for his moral and political ideas. The following account focuses on the moral, rather than the political, issues of Locke's account. You are encouraged to enquire for yourself whether Locke's or Hobbes's position is more convincing.

Locke's State of Nature

There are a number of similarities between Locke's and Hobbes's descriptions of the state of nature. For the present, we will focus only on two of these. In the first case, both philosophers claim that individuals within the state of nature are free and equal. Second, both claim that there is a law of nature that governs individuals within the state of nature. Despite these similarities, however, there are important differences in their accounts that reveal contrasting views of morality.

Both Hobbes and Locke claim that the state of nature is one of freedom and equality. Individuals in the state of nature, Locke says, are in a state of '*perfect freedom* to order their actions, and dispose of their possessions and persons, as they think fit'.[6] In addition, Locke says it is a '*state* also of *equality*, wherein all the power and jurisdiction is reciprocal, no one having more than another'.[7] What Locke means by freedom and equality, however, is not the same as Hobbes. While Hobbes claims individuals are free to perform any action they believe will advance their own self-preservation, Locke claims there are moral limits to human actions. 'But though this be a *state of liberty*', Locke says, 'yet *it is not a state of licence*: though man in that state have an uncontrollable liberty to dispose of his person or possessions, yet he has not liberty to destroy himself, or so much as any creature in his possession, but where some nobler use than its bare preservation calls for it.'[8] For Locke, human equality is the foundation for these moral limits since there is 'nothing more evident, than that creatures of the same species and rank, promiscuously born to all the same advantages of nature, and the use of the same faculties, should also be equal one amongst another without subordination or subjection'[9]. As we have seen, Hobbes believes 'equality' is a descriptive term that refers to the equal ability to kill others. Locke, on the other hand, holds that individuals are equal insofar as they deserve a certain kind of treatment or respect. In other words, 'equality' is a descriptive term (i.e., a term that says what 'is' the case) for Hobbes and a prescriptive term (i.e., a term that says what 'ought' to be the case) for Locke.

The differences between Locke's and Hobbes's moral views are also seen in their contrasting views on the law of nature. Locke offers two reasons for the existence of a natural moral law, one theological and the other non-theological. First, Locke claims that human equality and independence offers grounds for the existence of certain natural rights: 'The *state of nature* has a law of nature to govern it, which obliges every one: and reason, which is that law, teaches all mankind, who will but consult it, that being all *equal and independent*, no one ought to harm another in his life, health, liberty, or possessions'.[10] Second, Locke claims that we are God's creatures and, for this reason, we should not use other people simply for our own purposes. '[F]or men being all the workmanship of one omnipotent, and infinitely wise maker', Locke says, 'they are his property, whose workmanship they are, made to last during his, not one another's pleasure: and being furnished with like faculties, sharing all in one community of nature, there cannot be supposed any such *subordination* among us, that may authorize us to destroy one another, as if we were made for another's uses'[11]. Locke strongly implies here that we should not harm or subordinate others in the state of nature because it is *morally wrong* given that we are equal and God's property. Although Locke claims we should not harm others in the state of nature, he also says that there are some circumstances in which it is right to do so, namely, in order to punish those who break the law of nature. Significantly, however, there are limits to punishment; transgressors of the natural law 'may be *punished* to the degree, and with so much *severity*, as will suffice to make it an ill bargain to the offender, give him cause to repent, and terrify others from doing the like'.[12] In his account of the law of nature, then, Locke provides a non-egoistic justification for morality. For Locke, in other words, the law of nature gives us an objective and natural standard of moral behaviour; it tells people what is right or wrong by nature. Conversely, Hobbes says that the law of nature prohibits us from harming others because we will ultimately hurt ourselves by doing so (at least according to one interpretation of Hobbes).

Moral Relativism and Moral Absolutism

The primary question raised here is whether there are any natural objective standards that may be used to assess the morality of human actions. Is it the case that slavery is objectively wrong? Or is it wrong only because it is accepted as wrong? Is there a sense of justice that transcends the laws of individual states and nations? Or is morality created by human laws and agreements? To answer these questions, you must consider the condition of morality in a state of nature. In such a state, does anything go? Or are there natural limits to human behaviour? If, for example, I spend a day in the state of nature catching fish from a stream, would it be *morally wrong* for another man to steal the fish from me to preserve himself? For Locke, the work and effort that I put into this task would turn the fish into my property: I would have a natural (and exclusive) right to the fish. For Hobbes, however, each person has a natural right to all things, so that other people would equally be able to claim a right to the fish. Whose position is the correct one? Why?

CONCLUSION

In this chapter, the summary of Hobbes's moral philosophy revealed that he holds the following beliefs about morality: (1) there are no objective standards of morality in the state of nature; (2) the state of nature is a state of war; (3) the laws of nature provide the means to peace and self-preservation; (4) the laws of nature prohibit what is traditionally considered immoral behaviour. After the summary, an interpretative conflict over Hobbes's laws of nature was presented. As we have seen, there seems to be evidence for two incompatible interpretations of the laws of nature. First, the laws of nature are prudential precepts that reveal rational means for individuals to pre-serve themselves. Second, the laws of nature are genuine moral laws because they are commanded by God.

The last section of the chapter initiated an enquiry into moral issues by contrasting Locke's and Hobbes's respective views of the state of nature.

CHAPTER 5

HOBBES'S POLITICAL PHILOSOPHY

Political philosophy raises questions about the origin and legitimacy of political institutions and the rights and duties of both citizens and rulers: What is the ultimate source of political authority? Who should wield political power? What are the respective rights and duties of citizens and leaders? When is civil disobedience justified? What is the origin of the commonwealth? Hobbes tries to answer such questions in his works on political philosophy. For Hobbes, political philosophy is not simply an interesting intellectual pursuit; it also carries important practical consequences. As mentioned in the first chapter, Hobbes was witness to a civil war that was ripping his country apart. Various political and religious leaders had different ideas about who should possess political power and how it should be used. Such ideological disagreements did not remain confined to the realm of ideas, but created conflict in the real world. Hobbes believed that his own political philosophy, if accepted, would help produce and maintain a state of peace. According to Hobbes, humans could escape from civil war, metaphorically represented by the 'state of nature', only by accepting a sovereign with absolute power. In this chapter, you will be introduced to the main elements of Hobbes's political philosophy. As we will see, Hobbes believes that the transition from the state of nature to an organized political settlement occurs when individuals make a political covenant with each other. While a political covenant might lead to any one of a number of forms of government, Hobbes believes peace requires the institution of an absolute sovereign – a ruler – who has the final say on all ethical, religious and political matters. In the second section, an interpretative problem concerning Hobbes's political absolutism will be presented. Although Hobbes advocates political absolutism, some scholars claim that he implicitly accepts the notion of a limited sovereign. After examining this issue for yourself, you can decide whether this claim is reasonable. The chapter concludes with an enquiry into ideas about the rights of governments to limit their subjects' liberties. How far should a government go in protecting us from each other? How much liberty should be granted to each citizen? What justifies the governmental limitations on the liberty of citizens?

I. SUMMARY: HOBBES'S POLITICAL PHILOSOPHY

The Political Covenant[1]

The purpose of instituting a government, according to Hobbes, is to escape from the warlike conditions of the state of nature. As we saw in the last chapter, Hobbes believes that the state of nature, a hypothetical state void of laws and institutions of legal enforcement, is equivalent to war. In Hobbes's view, people in the state of nature have a natural right to do whatever *they believe* is necessary for their own preservation. If I believe, for example, that killing you is necessary for my survival, then I have a natural right to kill you. As long as people retain this natural right, Hobbes argues, they will remain in that 'miserable condition of war' where everyone is a threat to everyone else (*L* 17.223). To escape from the state of nature, however, people must not only give up the natural right to decide for themselves what is or is not necessary for their own preservation, but they must transfer this right to one individual, or a group of individuals, who will then act for the benefit of the whole. The transfer of this right to a common power, Hobbes says, is 'made by a covenant of every man with every man, in such manner, as if every man should say to every man, "I authorize and give up my right of governing myself to this man or to this assembly of men"'(*L* 17.227). Individuals, in other words, make a *political covenant* with each other to transfer their right of governing themselves to a common authority, that is, the sovereign power. A state of security and peace emerges from the political covenant, according to Hobbes, because the sovereign is authorized to use its newly acquired power and strength not only to enact and enforce laws, but also to defend the commonwealth against enemies. The 'depravity of the human disposition', Hobbes says, is such that people will follow laws or fight for others only when it suits their interests, thus the threat of punishment is required to encourage behaviour that is good for the commonwealth (*Ci* 6.176). 'Consent', Hobbes says, 'is not sufficient security for their common peace, without the erection of some common power, by the fear whereof they may be compelled both to keep the peace amongst themselves and to join their strengths together against a common enemy' (*El* I.19.6).

By means of a political covenant, Hobbes says, people create a 'mortal God' to protect themselves not only from each other, but also from foreign invaders.

> This is the generation of that great leviathan, or rather (to speak more reverently) of that *mortal God*, to which we owe under the *immortal God*, our peace and defense. For by this authority, given him by every particular man in the commonwealth, he has the use of so much power and strength conferred on him, that by terror thereof, he is enabled to form the wills of them all to peace at home and mutual aid against their enemies abroad (*L* 17.227–8).

While the comparison of the sovereign to God may seem to be hyperbolic, it expresses an important point that the sovereign has unquestioned authority. As we shall see in Chapter 6, Hobbes believes that God exists outside the realm of human morality and is incapable of doing an unjust act. In a similar manner, the sovereign's actions cannot be judged unjust. One rationale for this point is found in the interesting fact that the sovereign is not a contracting party in the political covenant. Individuals in the state of nature make a covenant with everyone else to institute a sovereign. The sovereign is just a third party. An important consequence of this fact is that the sovereign cannot be accused of being unjust because, as we saw in Chapter 4, injustice is the breaking of a covenant. In the state of nature, prior to the making of agreements, there is no justice or injustice. By being a third party outside the political covenant, then, the sovereign essentially remains in a state of nature and retains the natural right to all things. Because the sovereign is basically above moral judgement, the comparison with God is apt.

The political covenant, Hobbes says, creates an 'artificial person' who becomes the 'actor' for the 'people' as a whole. Hobbes defines a person as someone 'whose words or actions are considered either as his own or as representing the actions of another man' (*L* 16.217).

A person, when acting for other people, is considered to be 'artificial'. A 'natural person', on the other hand, acts for his or her own self. When individuals in a state of nature institute a sovereign through the political covenant, they create an artificial person whose actions are the actions of the 'people'. In Hobbes's terminology, the institution of a sovereign power represents a transition from a 'multitude' of individuals in a state of nature to a real 'unity' of citizens in a commonwealth. Each citizen in a commonwealth, Hobbes argues, must therefore recognize that the sovereign's actions are really his or her own. Thus, if the sovereign makes a covenant as a representative of the people, the people themselves are bound by the covenant as if they themselves made it. In fact, the people are obliged by any covenant made by the sovereign because, as Hobbes says, they authorized the sovereign to act on their behalf. 'From hence it follows', Hobbes says, 'that when the actor makes a covenant by authority, he binds the author no less than if he had made it himself' (*L* 16.218).

PERPLEXING PROBLEM: THE PROBLEM OF LAYING DOWN RIGHTS

A perplexing problem arises when one juxtaposes the following two claims made by Hobbes: (1) that a sovereign is instituted by a 'mutual transfer of right' and (2) the sovereign has the 'power and strength' to create a state of peace. The problem arises because individuals in a political covenant do not technically transfer any of their power to the sovereign, but simply transfer the right to rule themselves. As we have seen, individuals in the state of nature institute a sovereign by *transferring* the right to govern themselves to a third party. Transferring one's rights, however, is just one method of 'laying down one's rights'. When a person 'lays down' a right, Hobbes says, 'he divests himself of the liberty of hindering another of the benefit of his own right to the same' (*L* 14.190). For example, if I 'lay down' my right to fish in the river, then I oblige myself not to hinder others from fishing. I do not, however, 'confer' on you my strength and power to help you fish. Hobbes says that the sovereign is instituted by a *transfer* of right; according to the definition of laying down rights, however, such a transfer does not transfer power. When I make a political covenant, technically speaking, I agree *not to hinder* the sovereign from exercising his or her power.

In the transfer of right, I do not agree to help the sovereign. How, then, does the sovereign acquire the power and strength necessary to enforce laws or to protect the commonwealth from foreign enemies? How might Hobbes respond to this question?

Valid and Invalid Covenants

The third law of nature, as we have seen, demands that individuals follow through on their covenants. If people do not obey this law of nature, Hobbes says, then the political covenant will falter and individuals will return to the state of nature. The only way for the commonwealth to succeed is for the citizens to abide by the decisions of the sovereign. The political covenant, in other words, includes the agreement to obey the sovereign. If individuals decide to break the civil law, they are breaking the political covenant; but no commonwealth can survive if its citizens are constantly breaking the laws. In fact, peace requires individuals to abide by all covenants made, not just the political one. Thus, only 'fools' would intentionally break their covenants (see the 'Problem of the Fool' in Chapter 4). There are some cases, however, where covenants are invalidated; in such cases, Hobbes says, it is reasonable for a person not to fulfil his or her end of the bargain. For example, in the state of nature, if one of the parties in a covenant has a reasonable suspicion that the other party will not perform, then the covenant becomes void. This reasonable suspicion must arise after the covenant has been made; if a person has a reasonable suspicion before making the covenant and still makes it, then the covenant is still binding. In a state of nature, the ability to void a contract is necessary in cases of reasonable suspicion because individuals need to protect themselves from greedy and avaricious people. 'For he that performs first has no assurance the other will perform after', Hobbes says, 'because the bonds of words are too weak to bridle man's ambition, avarice, anger, and other passions' (*L* 14.196). In other words, words and promises (in the state of nature) are not enough to ensure that the other party will fulfil the covenant since there are no means of enforcement. If, however, two parties in a covenant live under a sovereign with coercive power, then a reasonable suspicion that the other party will not perform *does not* invalidate the covenant.

Some covenants, Hobbes says, will always be void. For example, 'a covenant not to defend myself from force by force is always void'

(*L* 14.199). If my life is threatened, in other words, I have the right to defend myself. In addition, there are certain kinds of covenants that are invalid by their nature because, technically speaking, they are not covenants. For example, it is not possible to make covenants with animals because they cannot understand our language. Likewise, humans cannot covenant with God unless He speaks to them through divine revelation or through a representative. There must be some confirmation, in other words, that God has accepted the covenant. Hobbes also says that covenants must be concerned with *possible* actions. I cannot promise you everlasting life in exchange for your money since it is not possible for me to give you eternal life.

Interestingly, Hobbes claims that 'covenants entered into by fear, in the condition of mere nature, are obligatory' (*L* 14.198). For example, if I am forced at gunpoint to promise to kill another individual tomorrow in order to save my own life today, then I am obliged to kill that individual, even if my own life is not immediately threatened tomorrow. Even in a civil state, an individual is obliged to follow through on covenants made out of fear unless the civil law says otherwise. Hobbes's claim here seems to be in direct contrast with the principle of responsibility, which is a commonly accepted moral principle. As mentioned in Chapter 4, most people would accept the view that moral obligation requires a certain level of freedom. For example, if I am forced at gunpoint to promise to kill the president tomorrow, most people would say that I am not bound to fulfil my promise since I was forced, out of fear for my own life, to make that promise. In part, Hobbes believes that contracts made out of fear are not void because the political covenant to establish a sovereign is made out of fear. Individuals in a state of nature covenant with each other, out of fear for their own lives, to create a state of peace by the institution of a sovereign power. If covenants made out of fear were void, then the political covenant itself would be invalid.

PERPLEXING PROBLEM: THE PROBLEM OF ESCAPING THE STATE OF NATURE

Hobbes claims that one party of a covenant may rightfully break it in the state of nature if there is 'reasonable suspicion' that the other party is not going to perform its part. According to Hobbes, this 'reasonable suspicion' must be based upon some new information that is acquired after the covenant has been made. At first, this seems quite reasonable. Imagine, for example, that you covenant with another person in the state of nature to work together on a common project. You later discover, however, that this person has broken previous covenants with others. Reasonably, as a means to protect yourself from a covenant-breaker, you decide to ignore the requirements of your own covenant. According to Hobbes, you would be right to do so. However, a problem arises because of an ambiguity in the phrase 'reasonable suspicion'. In the state of nature, Hobbes says, each person must determine for him- or herself what is or is not reasonable. Recall that the state of nature is a state of war where 'everyone is an enemy of everyone'. In such a state, might not a 'reasonable suspicion' continually arise that others will not fulfil their covenants? How is a political covenant possible in such a state? Will not political covenants be voided almost immediately by the 'reasonable suspicion' that one's enemies will not abide by their agreements? Is this a real problem for Hobbes?

The Specific Rights of the Sovereign Power

Since the sovereign power is instituted to maintain a state of peace and security in the commonwealth, Hobbes argues that the sovereign must possess certain rights to fulfil its assigned function.[2] In *Leviathan*, Hobbes specifically lists 12 rights that are 'incommunicable and inseparable' from sovereignty (*L* 18.236). It is worth looking at a few of these in detail. The first right is the sovereign's right not to be dispossessed of its power and authority by means of a new political covenant. If the subjects of a commonwealth believe that the sovereign power is not acting for the common good, for example, it would be unjust for them to covenant to form a new government. Hobbes derives this sovereign right from the third law of nature, which, as we saw in the previous chapter, states that people must not break their covenants. According to Hobbes, 'they that have already instituted a commonwealth, being thereby bound by Covenant, to own the actions and judgments of one, cannot lawfully make a new covenant amongst themselves to be obedient to any other, in any thing whatsoever, without his permission' (*L* 18.229). To make a new covenant would be to break the original covenant, which would be unjust.

Hobbes also claims that the sovereign has the right not to be accused of acting unjustly by a subject since the citizen is technically the author of the sovereign's actions. For example, if I believe I am the victim of sovereign injustice, I should not accuse the sovereign; rather, I should recognize that I am responsible for the sovereign's actions, as if I were the one performing them. For Hobbes, this leads to the interesting and seemingly paradoxical claim that it is *logically impossible* for a subject to accuse the sovereign of *injustice*. According to Hobbes, while it is possible for one to hurt oneself, it is not possible to act unjustly towards oneself since one does not covenant with oneself. 'He that complains of injury from his sovereign', Hobbes says, 'complains of that whereof he himself is the author and therefore ought not to accuse any man but himself; no nor himself of injury because to do injury to oneself is impossible' (*L* 18.232). It should be noted that Hobbes uses 'injury' here as a synonym for 'injustice' and not 'harm'.

The sovereign, in Hobbes's view, has the sole right to determine which doctrines and opinions may be held in the commonwealth. 'It belongs therefore to him that hath sovereign power', Hobbes says, 'to be judge, or constitute all judges of opinions and doctrines, as a thing necessary to peace, thereby to prevent discord and civil war' (*L* 18.233). Hobbes says that religious beliefs are especially important for the sovereign to control. As we shall see in the next chapter, religious doctrines are frequently responsible for serious discord in the commonwealth, according to Hobbes, because people use God's word to question the sovereign's actions. A state of peace requires a civil authority with the right to determine religious doctrines so that religion and politics do not clash. 'There was no such dilemma [of civil conflict] among the Jews', Hobbes says, because 'the interpreters [of the Old Testament] whereof were the priests, whose power was subordinate to the power of the king' (*El* II.6.2). If the sovereign has the power to interpret holy texts, Hobbes claims, then individuals cannot use their religious beliefs to stir up rebellion.

In addition to these three rights, Hobbes reveals nine other rights of the sovereign including, among others, the right to enact and enforce all laws, to choose when to declare war and to judge all disputes between citizens. Taken as a whole, the sovereign rights entail a position known as 'political absolutism', which grants absolute power to the sovereign in all matters political, religious and ethical. It should be emphasized, of course, that the sovereign does not personally have to make every law, judgment, or decision related to the commonwealth. Instead, the sovereign is in charge of appointing, and replacing when necessary, the legislators, counsellors, judges and ministers of the state. To those who believe that granting such absolute power is too dangerous, Hobbes has the following response.

> And though of so unlimited a power, men may fancy many evil consequences, yet the consequences of the want of it, which is perpetual war of every man against his neighbor, are much worse. The condition of men in this life shall never be without inconveniences; but there happens in no commonwealth any great inconvenience but what proceeds from the subjects' disobedience and breach of those covenants from which the commonwealth has its being (*L* 20.260).

Without an absolute sovereign, Hobbes argues, the state will necessarily dissolve into a war of all against all. Thus, it is better to accept the inconveniences of political absolutism than the terrors of civil war.

Absolutism or War?

Individuals in the state of nature, Hobbes says, must choose one of two options; they may decide to remain in a state of nature and risk their lives in a war of all against all, or they may decide to live under an absolute ruler and accept the accompanying 'inconveniences'. The third option of a limited sovereign power does not exist for Hobbes. In his view, it is impossible to have a limited ruler because there must always be one ultimate source of political power. Hobbes advances here the 'regress argument for absolute sovereignty', which may be stated as follows.[3]

1. Either a ruler's power is limited or it is unlimited.
2. If it is limited, then there must be a higher power that limits the ruler.
3. This higher power is either limited or unlimited.
4. If it is limited, there must be a power greater than this 'higher power'.
5. This regress of powers cannot go on forever.
6. Thus, if the ruler's power is limited, it must ultimately be limited by an unlimited power.

7. Thus, either the ruler's power is unlimited or it is limited by an unlimited power (which is the real ruler).

For Hobbes, a government with divided powers will necessarily falter because, as the saying goes, 'a kingdom divided in itself cannot stand' (L 18.236). The civil war in England, Hobbes says, is evidence for his position. In his view, the belief that the king and parliament should share political power ultimately led to civil war. 'If there had not first been an opinion received of the greatest part of England, that these powers were divided between the King, and the Lords, and the House of Commons', Hobbes says, 'the people had never been divided and fallen into this civil war' (L 18.236–7).

PERPLEXING PROBLEM: THE PROBLEM OF AUTHORIZATION

Hobbes's political absolutism entails, among other things, the notion that the people cannot recall their rights once transferred to the sovereign. When individuals in a state of nature transfer their rights in the political covenant, Hobbes claims that the transfer is irrevocable. As some Hobbes scholars point out, however, this notion of 'alienating' one's rights (i.e., completely giving them up) seems to be incompatible with the notion of authorization.[4] If I authorize you to act on my behalf, in other words, you are simply the actor while I maintain the authority. Conceptually speaking, then, authorization seems to imply that I have the authority to choose another person to act on my behalf. 'If the subjects authorize the sovereign', it has been asked, 'why cannot the subjects de-authorize him?'[5] How do you think Hobbes would respond to this question?

Civil Laws and Political Absolutism

The legislation and enforcement of civil laws are the means by which the sovereign is able to maintain peace within the commonwealth. Law, generally speaking, is a command issued by a proper authority by which rules of conduct are established. More specifically, the civil law 'is to every subject, those rules which the commonwealth has commanded him . . . to make use of, for the distinction of right and wrong' (L 26.312). In his treatment of the nature of civil law, Hobbes confirms his commitment to political absolutism in two important ways. In the first case, Hobbes argues that the sovereign is above the civil law because the person with the authority to make or repeal law cannot be subject to it. The sovereign, Hobbes says, 'is not subject to the civil law' since 'having the power to make and repeal laws, he may when he pleases, free himself from subjection by repealing those laws that trouble him' (*L* 26.313). In the second case, Hobbes wants to ensure that the sovereign's authority over law cannot be called into question by a creative interpretation. As Hobbes points out, the sovereign might make a law that is subject to a variety of interpretations. (Having read Hobbes, you should understand this point well!) A 'crafty' rabble-rouser could therefore interpret a civil law in a manner that is contrary to the intentions of the sovereign (*L* 26.322). What is important, Hobbes says, is not the letter of the law, but the spirit, i.e., what the sovereign intended. Thus, it is important that the sovereign is the interpreter of the law as well. One should not be able to use a creative interpretation of the sovereign's law against the sovereign.

PERPLEXING PROBLEM: THE PROBLEM OF THE CIVIL LAWS AND THE LAWS OF NATURE

Hobbes claims the civil law and the laws of nature 'contain each other' and are of 'equal extent' (*L* 26.314). Prior to the formation of the commonwealth, Hobbes says, the laws of nature are not genuine laws, but are simply 'qualities' that lead individuals towards the moral life. As we saw in Chapter 4, there is a debate about whether the laws of nature are genuine moral laws commanded by God. In a very interesting passage, a passage that may confuse this issue even further, Hobbes suggests that the sovereign converts the laws of nature into civil laws.

> The laws of nature and the civil law contain each other and are of equal extent. For the laws of nature, which consist in equity, justice, gratitude, and other moral virtues on these depending, in the condition of mere nature . . . are not properly laws, but qualities that dispose men to peace and to obedience. When a commonwealth is once settled, then they are actually laws and not before, as being the commands of the commonwealth and therefore also the civil laws. For it is the sovereign power that obliges men to obey them (*L* 26.314).

legitimate laws

The basic point here is that the laws of nature are not enforced by a coercive power (unless one considers God to be the enforcer) and so humans are not bound to follow them. After the formation of a commonwealth, according to Hobbes, the laws of nature become obligatory because they become part of the civil law. Civil laws, then, ultimately command the same things as the laws of nature. In addition, Hobbes further claims that 'obedience to the civil law is part also of the natural law' (L 26.314). Thus, the civil law is part of the law of nature and the law of nature is part of the civil law. What exactly does this mean? Is it not possible for a civil law to go against a law of nature? How might Hobbes answer these questions?

The Superiority of Monarchy

It should be emphasized that one or more people may hold the sovereign power. The notion of political absolutism, in other words, should not be confused with monarchy. In Hobbes's view there are three forms of government that are distinguished by the number of rulers in a commonwealth. Monarchy is the rule of one; aristocracy is the rule of many; democracy is the rule of all. According to Hobbes, monarchy is superior to both aristocracy and democracy. Hobbes's general reasoning is that monarchy is superior to the other forms because political problems are more likely to arise if political authority is divided among two or more people. For example, as Hobbes points out, leaders are not only political representatives, but are also human beings with their own wants and desires. In cases where political representatives must choose between advancing their own interests or the interests of the whole, Hobbes believes that they will choose their own. 'And though he be careful in his political person to procure the common interest', Hobbes says, 'yet he is more or no less careful to procure the private good of himself, his family, kindred and friends; and for the most part, if the public interest chance to cross the private, he prefers the private' (L 19.241). In a monarchy, Hobbes argues, the monarch prospers only if the citizens prosper. By contrast, in other forms of government, Hobbes claims that members of assemblies often seek their own good at the expense of the commonwealth. As another example, Hobbes claims that political representatives will be more concerned for 'flatterers' and family members than for the ordinary citizen. This 'inconvenience' will be minimized in a monarchy, Hobbes claims, where only one person does this.

96

Commonwealth by Acquisition

In the previous sections, we discussed what Hobbes calls a 'commonwealth by institution'. In this kind of commonwealth, the sovereign originally acquires the rights of sovereignty when individuals in a state of nature covenant with each other to institute a sovereign. There is, however, another origin of sovereign power. In a 'commonwealth by acquisition', Hobbes says, the sovereign power is not acquired by means of a political covenant among individuals. Instead, it is won by an act of force as when, for example, a sovereign invades and conquers a foreign country. In both kinds of commonwealths, however, there is still a sort of covenant based on fear. Sovereignty by acquisition, according to Hobbes, 'differs from sovereignty by institution only in this, that men who choose their sovereign do it for fear of one another, and not of him whom they institute: But in this case [of sovereignty by acquisition], they subject themselves to him they are afraid of' (*L* 20.252). In a commonwealth by acquisition, those conquered *freely choose* to be ruled by the conqueror out of fear for their lives. Because individuals make a free choice, the rights of sovereigns by acquisition are supposedly identical to those of sovereigns by institution. As we saw in Chapter 4, Hobbes believes that coerced decisions are still considered 'free' unless individuals are physically restrained or incapacitated. Covenants made out of fear, in other words, are still obligatory in Hobbes's opinion. If they were not, then even the citizens in a commonwealth by institution would not be obliged by their covenant because it is made out of fear of each other. In a commonwealth by acquisition, it 'is not therefore the victory that gives right of dominion over the vanquished, but his own covenant' (*L* 20.255-6). The rights of the sovereign, therefore, are the same in both kinds of commonwealths and for the same reasons.

The Rights of Subjects

In the state of nature, as we saw in Chapter 4, individuals possess the natural right to do whatever they believe is necessary to ensure their own preservation. According to Hobbes, however, individuals must relinquish this right of self-governance in order to establish a state of peace. 'For as long as every man holds this right of doing anything he likes', Hobbes says, 'so long are men in the condition of

laws of nature vs civil law

war' (*L* 14.190). Individuals transfer this right to a common power, Hobbes claims, primarily to ensure their own good, especially their own survival. Thus, subjects of a sovereign power have accepted a limitation of their natural rights in exchange for the benefits of life in a peaceful commonwealth. Despite this limitation of right, Hobbes says that 'there be some rights which no man can be understood by any words, or any other signs, to have abandoned or transferred' (*L* 14.192). Since each desires his or her own good, certain rights must be retained to guarantee personal security; these rights cannot be forfeited. For example, a person 'cannot lay down the right of resisting them, that assault him by force, to take away his life', Hobbes claims, 'because he cannot be understood to aim thereby at any good to himself' (*L* 14.192). Interestingly, this right of resistance is held even if the attackers have justice on their side. So, for instance, if the sovereign commands an individual not to resist attackers, the individual has the right to disobey. Hobbes describes other specific situations in which a person maintains a right to disobey the sovereign's order; these situations are covered under the following general principle: 'When, therefore, our refusal to obey frustrates the end for which the sovereignty was ordained, then there is no liberty to refuse; otherwise, there is' (*L* 21.269). Hobbes, in other words, believes that an individual has the right to disobey the sovereign's orders if such disobedience does not prevent the sovereign from accomplishing intended goals. If, for example, the sovereign commands me to kill a guilty man, I have the right to disobey if I can find another person to do the job for me. The greatest source of a subject's liberties, however, is found in the silence of the law. 'As for other liberties', Hobbes says, 'they depend on the silence of the law. In cases where the sovereign has prescribed no rule, there the subject has the liberty to do, or forbear, according to his own discretion' (*L* 21.271). If an act is not against the law, in other words, it is permitted.

II. INTERPRETATION: DOES HOBBES IMPLICITLY ACCEPT A LIMITED SOVEREIGN?

In this section, we will explore an interpretative problem regarding Hobbes's political absolutism. On the one hand, Hobbes clearly advocates an absolutist view that gives the sovereign the last word on political matters. On the other hand, Hobbes implies that subjects in a commonwealth have the final say. The interpretative question, to put it another way, is whether Hobbes really adheres to political absolutism or actually accepts the notion of a sovereign with limited power. The conflict of interpretation arises from the difference between what Hobbes wants to say and what he implies. As you read about this conflict, I suggest that you try to determine if there is a way to make what Hobbes says fit with what he implies.

A Limited Government?

In the Summary section, we saw evidence for the view that Hobbes adheres to political absolutism. Clearly, Hobbes intends to defend an absolutist form of government that ultimately places into the hands of the sovereign an inalienable right to use political power. While individuals in the state of nature exercise their own natural rights, once the covenant is made, Hobbes argues, the sovereign becomes the final arbiter on all matters. Despite his explicitly stated intentions, one might argue, Hobbes *implies* that the final source of political power really lies with the subjects. The basis for this implication is his claim that the subject has the right to disobey the sovereign when the latter is unable to protect the former. 'The obligation of subjects to sovereign is understood to last as long and no longer', Hobbes says, 'than the power lasts by which he is able to protect them' (*L* 21.272). In other words, if the sovereign cannot protect the subject from harm, then the subject may rightly disobey the sovereign. Yet, one may ask, who ultimately determines whether the sovereign genuinely provides protection? In answer to this question, Hobbes implies that the subject maintains the right to make the final decision: 'For the right men have by nature to protect themselves, when none else can protect them, can by no covenant be relinquished' (*L* 21.272). The implication here is that the *subject* cannot transfer the natural right to determine what promotes his or her self-preservation. If, for example, the sovereign passes a number of laws, which, in my opinion, threaten my life, would I not have the natural right to disobey these laws? It would seem that Hobbes must answer in the affirmative. Not only that, but Hobbes further implies that the subject not only retains the right to self-preservation, but also a right to a good life. 'As it is necessary for all men that seek peace, to lay down certain rights of nature', Hobbes claims, 'so it is necessary for man's life to retain some; as right to govern their own bodies; enjoy air, water, motion, ways to go from place to place; and all things else without which a man cannot live, or not live well' (*L* 15.212). Hobbes implies here that the subject maintains the right to 'live well' and so may justly disobey the sovereign in cases where the good life is threatened. If this is true, then it seems that the subjects of a commonwealth are the ultimate source of political right and power.

Passages to Consider
Comments and Questions on Passage 1

Passage 1 is taken from *Leviathan* immediately after Hobbes describes the sovereign's rights. In this passage, Hobbes takes issue with certain political thinkers who claim that kings or rulers, while having more power than any individual in a commonwealth, ultimately have less power than the individuals taken as a whole. A king may be above a particular subject, these thinkers say, but not above the whole people. Hobbes explains here why this opinion is 'absurd'. Does this passage rule out the notion that individual subjects do not have the right to determine when the sovereign has threatened them?

Passage 1
These are the rights which make the essence of sovereignty and which are the marks whereby a man may discern in what man, or assembly of men, the sovereign power is placed and resides . . . This great authority being indivisible, and inseparably annexed to the sovereignty, there is little ground for the opinion of them that say of sovereign kings, though they be *singulis majores*, of greater power than every one of their subjects, yet they be *universis minores*, of less power than them all together. For if by *all together*, they mean not the collective body as one person, then *all together*, and *every one* signifies the same and the speech is absurd. But if by *all together*, they understand them as one person (which the sovereign bears), then the power of all together is the same with the sovereign's power and so again the speech is absurd (*L* 18.236–7).

Comments and Questions on Passages 2 and 3

In Passage 2, Hobbes claims that individuals retain certain natural rights even after transferring most of them to the sovereign. More specifically, they retain the right to 'all things necessary to life'. The important question is: Who determines what is or is not necessary for a subject to live? According to Hobbes's psychological observations, 'all men by necessity of nature choose that to which to them appears to be the less evil' (*Ci* 6.5). Thus, it would seem that Hobbes believes that all humans will necessarily determine for themselves what is or is not evil to them. In Passage 3, however, Hobbes also claims that the sovereign is ultimately in charge of making this determination. Is there a way to interpret Passages 2 and 3 so that they complement each other?

Passage 2
As it was necessary that a man should not retain his right to every thing, so also was it that he should retain his right to some things: to his own body (for example) the right of defending, whereof he could not transfer; to the use of fire, water, free air, and place to live in, and to all things necessary to life. Nor does the law of nature command any divesting of other rights than of those only which cannot be retained without the loss of peace (*El* I.17.2).

Passage 3
It is also manifest that all voluntary actions have their beginning from and necessarily depend on the will; and that the will of doing or omitting aught, depends on the opinion of good and evil of the reward or punishment which a man conceives he shall receive by the act or omission: so as the actions of all men are ruled by the opinions of each. Wherefore, by evident and necessary inference, we may understand that it very much concerns the interests of peace that no opinions or doctrines be delivered to the citizens by which they may imagine that either by right they may not obey the laws of the city, that is, the commands of that man or council to whom the supreme power is committed, or that it is lawful to resist him, or that a less punishment remains for him that denies, than him that yields obedience . . . It follows therefore that this one, whether man or court, to whom the city has committed the supreme power, have also this right; that he both judge what opinions and doctrines are enemies to peace, and also that he forbid them to be taught (*Ci* 6.11).

Comments and Questions on Passage 4

In Passage 4, Hobbes discusses some of the specific situations in which individuals have the right to disobey the sovereign. The basic principle behind these situations is the subject's right to disobey in cases where such disobedience does not prevent the sovereign from completing intended goals. In these cases, the subject finds a substitute to perform the job. One might wonder, however, whether such justified disobedience could, in the long run, lead to an ineffective sovereign power. For example, if I disobey the sovereign's command to kill my mother because I found someone else to do it, am I not weakening the sovereign's power? What if the sovereign believes it is necessary for a peaceful state that sons must be willing to kill their parents in defence of the commonwealth? In such a case, would I still have the right to refuse?

Passage 4
If therefore I be commanded to kill myself, I am not bound to do it. For though I deny to do it, yet the right of dominion is not frustrated; since others may be found, who being commanded will not refuse to do it . . . Nor if he command to execute a parent, whether he be innocent or guilty and condemned by the law; since there are others who being commanded will do that and a son will rather die than live infamous and hated of all the world (*Ci* 6.13.183).

III. ENQUIRY: WHICH LIBERTY-LIMITING PRINCIPLES ARE JUSTIFIED?

One of the important questions in political philosophy is: What justifies the limitations placed on liberty through political force? According to Hobbes, individuals in a state of nature must relinquish some of their liberties in order to institute a sovereign power that will protect them. Such protection, one could say, is supposed to create a situation where individuals are secure enough to exercise whatever liberties they still naturally possess or are granted by law. Although it may seem paradoxical, the sovereign must limit or deny some of the rights of citizens to protect their rights to self-preservation. Many political philosophers agree that the purpose of government is to protect or promote some of the citizens' liberties precisely by restricting others. But which liberties should be protected and which should be limited? In attempting to answer this question, many political philosophers are guided by the 'basic principle of liberty', which states that individuals should be free to do whatever they wish unless there is a *justified reason* to restrict their freedom. But what constitutes a justified reason? What justification is there to limit some liberties over others? In many places, for example, individuals are required by law to wear seat belts but are not legally prevented from mountain climbing. By what principle is a government justified in threatening me with punishment if I do not wear a seat belt? In this section, we will look at some of the answers to such questions. More specifically, we will enquire into four different 'liberty-limiting principles': the harm principle, the offence principle, legal paternalism and legal moralism. As you read, you may consider the following questions: Which principles, if any, are you prepared to defend? Which principles ground your beliefs about what should be legal (or illegal)? Do you consistently apply these principles? Does your acceptance of a given principle depend upon the situation?

The Harm Principle

According to the *harm principle*, the liberty to perform certain actions may be justly restricted *only if* such actions cause harm to others. As John Stuart Mill claims, '[T]he only purpose for which power can be rightfully exercised over any member of a civilised community against his will, is to prevent harm to others. His own good, either physical or moral, is not a sufficient warrant.' For example, according to this principle, laws that deter people from intentionally torturing others just for fun would be considered justified. In addition, in enforcing the laws, a police officer would be right to use force to stop a man on a shooting spree in a mall. On the other hand, it would be unjust for a government to pass and enforce laws that prevent me from harming myself. Thus, the establishment and enforcement of seat belt laws would not be a justified use of government power according to the harm principle.

The harm principle appears to be well grounded at first sight. Yet further reflection leads to a number of interesting and perplexing questions. For example, what exactly does 'harm' mean? In cases such as rape and torture, it is obvious that a criminal causes *physical* harm to a victim. But what about other kinds of harm? Would a man cause harm to a woman by following her movements, calling her multiple times a day, or visiting her at work, against her wishes? Many people would agree that stalking constitutes harm and that governments are justified in forcefully stopping it. But where does this right come from? Is it because the man is causing *emotional* harm to the woman? If so, does a government have the general right to prevent emotional harm? Let's assume that I divorce my wife and leave my children against their wishes; am I not causing them emotional harm? It seems that I am. Is it just, therefore, for the government to make divorce or separation illegal? If not, what is the difference between the two cases? And further, let's assume that a peeping Tom takes photographs of his neighbour while she undresses, unbeknownst to her, and the photographs are never seen by anyone other than the voyeur. Is she being harmed in any way? If so, would a government be justified in stopping the peeping Tom?

The Offence Principle

The offence principle goes one step further than the harm principle by justifying the use of government power to prevent *offensive* actions. According to the offence principle, a person's liberties may be justly limited if such limitation prevents others from being offended. For example, this principle holds it is justified to make it illegal for a person to walk naked through a public park precisely because such an action is *offensive* to others. In determining what is offensive to others, the law must appeal to 'common standards of decency'. The offence principle, however, runs into the serious problem of trying to determine what counts as a common standard of decency. Is it simply a matter of putting it to a vote? Is something indecent if the majority of people say it is? And, if so, is it the majority of people in a given community, city or nation who decide standards of decency? In addition, the right to free speech often conflicts with the right not to be offended. So religious groups opposing abortion frequently and publicly display graphic posters of aborted foetuses. Such images, one might argue, are highly disturbing and, therefore, offensive. Should this take away their right to speak out against abortion in this manner?

Legal Moralism

Legal moralism holds that liberties may be justly restricted if such restriction prevents *immoral* actions. In many places, for example, homosexuality is outlawed primarily because it is considered immoral. Two people of the same sex engaged in a sexual act behind closed doors does not immediately affect others, thus this kind of action does not fall under the harm or offence principle; the

Does Hobbes engage n/ legal moralism?

purpose of these principles is to prevent actions that cause immediate harm or offence to other individuals. Legal moralism, by contrast, tries to stop immoral actions because such actions, it is argued, cause social erosion and threaten the health of the community. The belief that a goal of laws should be to create a moral society does raise serious questions. For example, whose moral opinions should be used to craft laws? Once again, does the majority decide what is or is not moral? If so, societies that accept the morality of slavery would be justified in using slaves. In addition, even if it were admitted by everyone that certain actions are immoral, should it be the purpose of government to prevent them? Let's assume that everyone agrees it is immoral for a man to tell his wife that he is going to work when, in actuality, he is going to play golf with his friends. Lying, of course, is an immoral action in most cases. If it becomes a common practice it will produce social discord. At what point is it just for a government to prevent lying or other immoral actions?

Legal Paternalism

While the other principles are primarily concerned with restricting an individual's liberties to protect others, legal paternalism is concerned with preventing harm to oneself. According to legal paternalism, it is just to restrict an individual's liberties if it will prevent harm to the person alone. It is commonly accepted that parents not only have the right, but the obligation, to do their best to prevent their children from harming themselves. Parents often restrict a child's liberty for his or her own good, even if the child strongly disagrees with the restriction. A two-year-old girl, for example, may desire to walk down a dangerous set of stairs unaccompanied, but a parent is right to stop her. Legal paternalists argue that the government's role is analogous to the parent's. Citizens must be protected, for their own good, from harming themselves. In a number of places, it is illegal to ride a bicycle without a helmet. In this case, the government tries to prevent the individual from performing an action that is directly harmful only to the individual. To what extent, one might ask, is it right for a government to take on a parental role? Should I not be allowed to snowboard, for example, even if it is dangerous? Should I be forced to wear a seat belt? Could this principle be used to regulate my eating habits?

Do You Consistently Apply Liberty-Limiting Principles?

Having been introduced to the liberty-limiting principles, it is time for you to consider whether you consistently apply these principles. Make a list of numerous laws that, in your opinion, justly limit a person's liberty. Then, try to determine which principle is at work in each case. Can you find an example of each principle? If you accept a principle in one case, why would you not accept it in another? For example, let's assume you believe that the government should prevent your neighbour from dropping his pants in front of your house every time he passes by. Is it not because you are offended by this action? And, if so, if you accept the offence principle in this case, why not accept it in all?

CONCLUSION

In this chapter, the summary of Hobbes's political philosophy revealed the following points: (1) the purpose of instituting a government is to escape from the dangerous state of nature; (2) the rights of the sovereign entail political absolutism; (3) individuals in the state of nature must ultimately choose to remain in the state of nature or accept to be ruled by an absolute sovereign; (4) monarchy is superior to other kinds of government; (5) a commonwealth acquired through conquest has the same legitimacy as an instituted government; (6) subjects maintain limited rights in a commonwealth, the most important of which is the right to protect oneself. After the summary, an interpretative problem concerning Hobbes's political absolutism was presented. As we have seen, there seems to be evidence that Hobbes undermines his political absolutism by suggesting that individuals, even in a commonwealth, must determine when their lives are endangered. In the enquiry section, questions concerning liberty-limiting principles were raised. As we have seen, one could argue that a government is justified in using force to curtail individual liberties if so doing will prevent people from harming or offending others, from performing immoral actions or from harming themselves.

CHAPTER 6

HOBBES'S PHILOSOPHY OF RELIGION

The philosophy of religion is the branch of philosophy that raises questions about God, the afterlife and the nature of our religious experience: Is there a God? What can we know about God? Why does God allow evil in the world? What duties and obligations, if any, does God impose upon us? Does God play an active role in the course of history? Does the soul exist after death? Such questions are not only philosophically relevant to Hobbes, but their answers have important political consequences. Hobbes lived during a time of serious religious controversy. The Protestant Reformation started in 1517 cast doubt on the Catholic Church's claims to being the only proper authority on Christian doctrine. Various religious leaders vied for the allegiance of the common people and political representatives and, as Hobbes would argue, tried to use their newly found influence to sway their followers away from lawful obedience to the king. Thus, Hobbes's view of religion has an immediate relevance to his political philosophy. In this chapter, we will investigate Hobbes's philosophy of religion. The first section provides a summary of Hobbes's philosophical views on God and religion. As we shall see, Hobbes believes that natural reason can be used to prove God's existence, but it cannot tell us much about His characteristics. In addition, Hobbes argues that the authority to determine religious doctrine should ultimately lie in the hands of the sovereign, for if this authority lay in another source, civil conflict would ultimately result. In the second section, you will be introduced to two different kinds of interpretation related to Hobbes's views on religion. According to some scholars, Hobbes's belief in God plays a minor role, if any, in the logic of his philosophical arguments. On the other hand, some scholars believe that God is at the heart of his philosophy. After considering the issues, you may decide for yourself which interpretation is more reasonable. The chapter concludes with an enquiry into the problem of evil. The main question raised in this section is: Why does a good and perfect God allow evil to exist in this world?

I. SUMMARY: HOBBES'S PHILOSOPHY OF RELIGION[1]

Faith and Reason

Information about God, according to Hobbes, is obtained from two sources: natural reason and the Holy Scriptures. Hobbes believes that both reason and scripture are given by God so that we can come to have knowledge of Him and His commands. Many religious believers, Hobbes included, are forced to question the relationship between reason and faith, especially when the two seem to come into conflict. For example, some Christians accept the notion of the Trinity, according to which there are three individual persons in one God: Father, Son and Holy Spirit. In this case, each person in the Trinity is not only one unique being, but is also identified with God himself. The idea that God is simultaneously one and three is an article of faith that seems to be contrary to reason. How is one thing the same as three things? Of course, one may try to make the idea of the Trinity comprehensible through a creative interpretation of it. For example, one could say that God is similar to one clover with three leaves. In this case, the Father, Son and Holy Spirit are three separate beings that are part of a God that is numerically one. Or, as another example, one may claim that the Trinity is similar to a family with three members, which could be considered one and three at the same time. Whether either explanation is a reasonable interpretation of a perplexing point of faith, I leave for you to decide. The general point here is that religious believers must decide for themselves what the relationship is between faith and reason. What happens when an article of faith cannot be reasonably explained? Must one adapt one's faith to fit reason or does one abandon reason and cling to faith? According to Hobbes, one must not reject reason in the attempt to understand God's word. 'For though there be many things in God's word above reason, that is to say, which cannot by natural reason either be demonstrated or confuted', Hobbes says, 'there is nothing contrary to it' (*L* 32.409–10). With the help of reason, a 'wise and learned interpretation of Scripture' may reveal 'all rules and precepts necessary to the knowledge of our duty both to God and man without enthusiasm or supernatural inspiration' (*L* 32.414). Of course, there are many parts of the Bible that are seemingly irrational or incomprehensible to us. In such cases, Hobbes says, 'the fault is either in our unskilful interpretation or erroneous ratiocination [reasoning]' (*L* 32.410). Faith and reason, according to Hobbes, are compatible, but in cases where they seem incompatible, the weakness of our reason is revealed.

Knowledge of God and His Laws through Reason

The power of reason, Hobbes says, is the 'natural word of God', given to us as a guide to 'justice, peace, and true religion' (*L* 32.409). As seen in Chapter 4, Hobbes points out that human reason discovers the laws of nature, which may be considered in one of two senses. On the one hand, natural laws are prudential precepts directing us towards self-preservation. On the other hand, natural laws are divine laws directing us towards the moral and political life. In addition to helping us understand God's laws, Hobbes believes that natural reason can be used to prove that God exists. Hobbes uses the 'first cause argument' to show that some eternal being must have started the motions of the universe. According to this argument, each event (or 'effect') in the natural universe is caused by a prior event (its 'cause'), which itself is an effect with a prior cause, and so on. Since this chain of events cannot reach into the past indefinitely, the argument goes, there must be a first cause that is responsible for getting it all started.

> For he that from any effect he sees come to pass, should reason to the next and immediate cause thereof, and from thence to the cause of that cause, and plunge himself profoundly in the pursuit of causes; shall at least come to this, that there must be (as even the heathen philosophers confessed) one first mover, that is, a first and eternal cause of all things, which is that which men mean by the name of God (*L* 12.170).

The first cause argument, of course, provides very little information about God's nature; it simply states that God set the natural world in motion. It does not tell us, for example, whether God plays any direct role in our lives.

Although Hobbes believes it is possible to prove that God exists, he says that human knowledge of God's other attributes is severely limited. 'For the nature of God', Hobbes says, 'is incomprehensible, that is to say, we understand nothing of what he is, but only that he is' (*L* 34.430). In this case, Hobbes adheres to a brand of 'negative theology', which is the view that we cannot say what God is, but only what He is not. We cannot, in other words, use positive adjectives to describe God, only negative ones. 'He that will attribute to God nothing but what is warranted by natural reason', Hobbes says, must 'use such negative attributes, as *infinite, eternal, incomprehensible*' (*L* 31.403). In other words, God is *not* finite, is *not* capable of death and is *not* comprehensible.

PERPLEXING PROBLEM: THE PROBLEM OF SPEAKING ABOUT GOD

According to Hobbes, we cannot really comprehend God's nature. Yet, Hobbes does not only just speak of God in terms of what He is not, but also in terms of what He is. For example, Hobbes claims that God is 'most high', 'just', 'holy' or 'good' (*L* 31.403). Is Hobbes caught in a contradiction on this matter? Hobbes says that any contradiction is only apparent because his descriptive words are used to *praise* God, rather than to *describe* God. There is a big difference, in other words, between a philosophical elucidation and a religious exaltation of God's attributes. Is Hobbes's response a good one?

Religion and Superstition

Religion and superstition, according to Hobbes's definitions, are defined as different kinds of fear. Hobbes defines religion, for example, as 'fear of power invisible, feigned by the mind or imagined from tales publicly allowed' (*L* 6.124). Superstition, Hobbes says, has the same definition as religion except that it ends with 'not publicly allowed'. These definitions are interesting for a number of reasons. In the first case, the idea that religion is a kind of fear might seem odd. The oddness dissipates, however, when one considers that Hobbes believes that religions originate because of fear. According to Hobbes, religious beliefs about divine beings arise because humans are naturally curious to know the reasons why good and bad things happen to them. Of course, in many cases the causes of such events are not immediately known and so humans naturally postulate the existence of 'invisible powers' that control or influence their fates. Out of fear of possible future evils, humans attempt to please these invisible powers through typical means of worship: presenting gifts, expressing reverence, good behaviour and so on. Thus, on account of fear (and lack of knowledge), religions and religious practices are established. The second interesting aspect of Hobbes's definitions of fear and superstition is the fact that the only difference is whether the civil law accepts or rejects the religious tales. So, for example, in a Christian nation whose sovereign does not allow Hindu stories of the Gods, such stories would be considered superstitious. But, if the Christian nation decides to allow Hindu stories, then they would cease to be superstitious. Perhaps because of this issue, Hobbes felt it necessary to define what a 'true' religion is. A religion is true, Hobbes says, 'when the power imagined is truly such as we imagine' (L 6.124). In other words, it would seem that the tales of a true religion accurately describe the 'invisible powers' that are ultimately in charge of our lives.

PERPLEXING PROBLEM: THE PROBLEM OF RELIGION AND SUPERSTITION

Hobbes's definitions of religion and superstition seem to present a problem because they imply that Christian beliefs would be superstitious if they were not allowed, as was the case in ancient Rome before Constantine. Hobbes, however, professes to be a Christian and so the veracity of his own religious belief seems to rely on whether they are allowed by the state. If it were the case, then, that Christian beliefs about the nature of God are accurate, then such beliefs could be simultaneously true and superstitious. If Hobbes lived under a sovereign who outlawed Christianity, would Christianity therefore be merely a superstition? How might Hobbes try to answer this question?

Religion and Politics

In his historical work *Behemoth*, Hobbes places much blame for the English Civil War on religious leaders. According to Hobbes, many religious leaders encouraged their followers to follow God, rather than the king, as if the king were leading them on a path away from

God. More specifically, Hobbes blames the Presbyterians, Papists (Catholics) and other religious groups who advocated freedom of religion. In Hobbes's view, Presbyterian preachers claimed to have a God-given right to govern the people, not only in their spiritual lives, but in their political ones. Hobbes complains that the Presbyterian preachers did not use reason or argument to convince people, but used tricks to captivate their audiences. In *Behemoth*, which is written in dialogue form, one of the characters claims that the mysterious actions of the preachers 'would have an effect on me to make me think them gods and to stand in awe of them as of God himself'.[2] It is also stated that many 'fruitless and dangerous doctrines' were accepted by the English people because they were 'terrified and amazed by preachers'.[3] It was in such a manner that the 'Presbyterian ministers, throughout the whole war, instigated the people against the King'.[4]

Hobbes does not just blame Presbyterians for stirring up civil unrest, but also Catholics. Hobbes claims that Catholics advanced the view that people should be governed by the pope, who is supposed to be God's representative on earth and the leader of all Christian people. Although popes did not directly challenge sovereign rulers, Hobbes says, they often used their 'spiritual power' to weaken the sovereign's 'temporal power'. The pope's spiritual power, according to Hobbes, consists of the power to excommunicate those who do not accept the points of faith established by the Catholic Church. Temporal power, on the other hand, supposedly belongs to the sovereign and it includes the power to judge and punish those who break the civil law. Popes, Hobbes says, are not content with being just spiritual leaders, so they extend their spiritual power to such a degree that it limits the king's temporal power. The most dangerous right claimed by the popes, Hobbes says, is the right of 'absolving subjects of their duties, and of their oaths of fidelity to their lawful sovereigns, when the Pope should think fit for the extirpation of heresy'.[5] The Papists, just like the Presbyterians, created situations of divided loyalty by infringing upon the temporal power of civil sovereignty. 'This power of absolving subjects of their obedience', Hobbes says, 'is as absolute a sovereignty as is possible to be and consequently there must be two kingdoms in one and the same nation, and no man be able to know which of the masters he must obey'.[6]

Hobbes also places some of the responsibility for the English Civil War on Independents, Anabaptists, Quakers and Adamites. These religious groups, according to Hobbes, were born from a 'controversy between the Papists and the Reformed Church that caused every man, to the best of his power, to examine by the Scriptures which of them was in the right'.[7] The ideological conflicts between Protestantism and Catholicism, in other words, caused many people to interpret the Bible on their own. On account of this, people believed that they could determine God's word for themselves. Such people, Hobbes says, 'thought they spoke with God Almighty and understood what He said'.[8] If people 'speak with God' directly, however, then each person may decide for him- or herself what civil laws are contrary to the law of God, giving them a reason to disobey the sovereign. Just as with the Presbyterians and the Catholics, Hobbes believes that these religious leaders caused political problems by creating situations of divided loyalty between God and king.

Even though Hobbes lived in a country and age where the vast majority of people professed to be Christians, there were still many debates concerning the truth of specific Christian doctrines. Hobbes claims that reason must be used skilfully to interpret the Holy Scriptures. But, one might ask, what counts as a 'skilful' interpretation of God's word? And further, what counts as God's word? Even though Christians agree that the Bible reveals the word of God, there is debate over which books of the Bible should be considered canonical. Another important question therefore arises: Who should have the authority to determine and interpret the Holy Scriptures? Hobbes considers four possible answers to this question: private individuals, prophets from God, established religious authorities (independent of the political state) or sovereigns. According to Hobbes, the fourth possibility is not only the most reasonable, but also the most politically practical.

If each person is responsible for interpreting God's word, Hobbes claims, situations of divided loyalty between God and sovereign are likely to arise. In many cases, people might see a conflict between the commands of God and those of the sovereign. Most people, including Hobbes, recognize that one should obey God's law when it conflicts with civil law. When the 'commands of God and men shall differ', Hobbes says, 'we are to obey God rather than man' (*El* II.6.2). In Chapter 4, we saw that individuals in a state of nature have the right to determine for themselves what is or is not conducive to their own preservation. We also saw that the retaining of this right leads to a state of war. Similarly, Hobbes believes, if individuals maintain their individual right to interpret God's word, then conflict and civil war will eventually follow. To avoid such a calamity, individuals must place the authority to interpret scripture into the hands of a third party. According to Hobbes, this third party must be the sovereign, not prophets or religious leaders. We should not appeal to prophets, Hobbes claims, because one cannot determine whether God has truly spoken to them. 'For if a man pretend to me that God has spoken to him supernaturally, and immediately, and I make doubt of it', Hobbes says, 'I cannot easily perceive what argument he can produce to oblige me to believe it' (*L* 32.411). Giving the authority of interpreting Scripture to religious leaders, such as the pope, is not a viable option since it, too, will produce civil discord in cases where the sovereign and the religious authority disagree. 'It may therefore be concluded the interpretation of all laws, sacred as well as secular, depends on the authority of the city, that is to say, that man or counsel to whom the sovereign power is committed' (*Ci* 15.305). This is the only possibility to avoid civil conflict based upon religious differences. In addition, it should be noted that Hobbes believes that citizens may privately believe whatever they wish about God, but they must publicly worship God in the manner decided upon by the sovereign power.

Hobbes's Interpretation of Scripture

In his works on political philosophy, and especially in *Leviathan*, Hobbes devotes a fair number of pages to the interpretation of Holy Scripture. One of the main goals of these interpretative passages is to show that the Bible supports, or is at least consistent with, his philosophical and political ideas. In *Leviathan*, for example, Hobbes tries to show how the various terms used in the Bible, such as 'spirit' and 'angel', are perfectly compatible with his materialist philosophy. In Hobbes's time, it was commonly accepted that 'incorporeal substances', such as souls or angels, exist in a realm outside the physical. As Hobbes sees it, natural reason tells us that all substances are corporeal, i.e., bodily. Thus, according to natural reason, the phrase 'incorporeal substance' is equivalent to the self-defeating phrase 'incorporeal body'. To support this conclusion of natural reason, Hobbes interprets a variety of biblical passages, sometimes with great creativity, in order to show that there is no evidence that incorporeal substances exist. In the Book of Genesis, for example, it is said that 'God made man of the dust of the earth and breathed into his nostrils the breath of life and man was made a living soul'. According to Hobbes's interpretation, the 'breath of life inspired by God signifies no more than that God gave him life' (*L* 34.432). The 'breath of life' and 'soul' do not necessarily refer to incorporeal entities, but could simply refer to very fine bodies that cannot be detected by sight. In a similar manner, Hobbes interprets biblical passages to show how they support, or are at least consistent with, his political absolutism. In his works on political philosophy, for example, Hobbes strings together numerous biblical passages to support the various political conclusions drawn by natural reason.

PERPLEXING PROBLEM: THE PROBLEM OF INTERPRETING GOD'S WORD

In all versions of his political philosophy, Hobbes clearly states that the sovereign must have the final word on religious doctrine and the interpretation of Scripture. In order to back up this claim, Hobbes frequently refers to the Holy Scriptures. One might wonder what Hobbes would think if the sovereign interpreted the Bible so that it conflicted with Hobbes's own view. For example, what if the sovereign claims, contrary to Hobbes's interpretation, that there is evidence in the Bible for the existence of incorporeal substances. How do you think Hobbes would respond?

God and Morality

In ancient Greece, Socrates raised the following question: Do the gods create the standards of morality or do the standards of morality exist independently of the gods? In a monotheistic Christian context we might ask whether God forbids murder because murder is wrong or whether murder is wrong because God forbids it. Religious philosophers, or at least those who believe in an all powerful and all good God, often struggle to find an adequate answer to this question because it raises an apparent conflict between God's power and His goodness. On the one hand, if God is omnipotent, one might say then God can do anything at all; He could, for example, command people to perform such immoral actions as rape and murder. If, on the other hand, God is completely benevolent, He could not perform or command an immoral act. Thus, one might argue, God cannot be both omnipotent and all good at the same time. Faced with this difficulty, religious thinkers must choose between emphasizing God's power or His goodness. Hobbes, accepting what is known as the 'divine command theory of morality', chooses to emphasize God's power over His goodness. According to this theory, God is responsible for creating the standards of morality which humans are naturally obliged to follow. Hobbes claims that God has a right to rule simply because of His immense power. 'God in his natural kingdom has a right to rule and to punish those who break his laws', Hobbes says, 'from his sole irresistible power' (*Ci* 15.292). It is not for us to question whether the laws or punishment are just or whether God's actions are just. Whatever God does is just, Hobbes says, simply because God does it. This position has obvious political consequences when one considers that earthly kings rule over citizens as God rules over His natural subjects. 'Legitimate kings', Hobbes says, 'make the things they command just by commanding them and those which they forbid, unjust, by forbidding them' (*Ci* 12.245). It is not hyperbole, as I suggested in Chapter 4, that God calls the sovereign the 'mortal God' on earth.

The divine command theory of morality provides Hobbes with a possible solution to a vexing problem for believers of an omnipotent and benevolent God, namely, the 'problem of evil'. The problem arises when one considers the existence of evil and suffering in this world. If God truly loves us and has the power to do anything, one might ask, why does He allow innocent people to suffer? This question, according to Hobbes, is basically the same as the question of what gives God the right to rule over us. 'That question made famous by the disputations of the ancients: why evil things befall the good, and good things the evil', Hobbes says, 'is the same with this of ours: by what right God dispenses good and evil things unto men' (*Ci* 15.293). As we have seen, Hobbes believes not only that God has a natural right to rule over us, but also that God's immense power justifies all of His actions. To illustrate this point, Hobbes refers to the biblical story of Job. After leading a truly pious life, Job complains to God of innumerable calamities that he has faced. In response, God asks Job: 'Where was thou when I laid the foundation of the earth?' According to Hobbes, God is justifying His 'punishment' of Job by appealing to His supreme power. While some might believe that God punishes Job for hidden sins, Hobbes does not. If God justified His punishment by reference to Job's sins, Hobbes claims, then God would be restricted by our moral standards. God, in other words, would use typically human moral concepts to explain and justify His actions. In this case, Job would be punished because he sinned. This explanation would fit with our moral standards. Hobbes believes that God's actions are just, however, not because they conform to our standards of morality, but simply because He performs them. Hobbes's solution to the problem of evil, then, is simply to say that God is not responsible for 'evil' because whatever he does is 'just', despite how it appears to us.

II. INTERPRETATION: DOES GOD PLAY A CENTRAL ROLE IN HOBBES'S PHILOSOPHY?

Interpreters of Hobbes differ greatly over the role of religious ideas in his philosophy. On the one hand, a number of Hobbes scholars disregard almost all of the religious elements in his thinking. Adherents of what is called the 'secular interpretation' claim, for one reason or another, that Hobbes's religious references are dispensable.[9] On the other hand, advocates of the 'religious interpretation' of Hobbes believe that God plays a central role in his philosophy.[10] It should be noted that these two categories of interpretation are generalizations that do not specify a detailed set of views; in each interpretation, there may be scholarly disagreement. So, for example, religious interpreters of Hobbes may have contrasting ideas about the role of God in his philosophy.

The Secular Interpretation

The common theme accepted by secular interpreters is that Hobbes should be read as a political, moral and natural philosopher. The primary goal of the secular interpreters is to show that Hobbes's moral and political philosophy does not rely on religious concepts or belief in God. Hobbes, it is argued, is first and foremost a *philosopher* concerned with advancing logical arguments that do not depend upon religious presuppositions. Hobbes himself claimed to have been the first philosopher to make a genuine 'science of politics'. Thus, it seems to follow that Hobbes believed the demonstration of his political and moral conclusions was free from religious beliefs. While the secular interpreters admit that Hobbes offers a traditional proof for God's existence, the proof does not reveal any important information about the divine being. In fact, Hobbes's 'negative theology' seems to make philosophical discussion about God pointless. For some secular interpreters, the main goal of *philosophical* interpretation is to analyse, evaluate and improve upon Hobbes's arguments for the sake of the arguments themselves. In this case, Hobbes's intentions are basically irrelevant. A less extreme position states that the proper interpretation of Hobbes's philosophy requires us to understand his intentions; nevertheless, when it comes to the relationship between Hobbes's religious and philosophical views, these interpreters claim that his theological beliefs about God are basically not important to his philosophical arguments. So, for example, secular interpreters often advocate the 'prudential interpretation' of the laws of nature. As discussed in Chapter 4, some interpreters claim that the laws of nature do not carry moral obligations. Instead, obligation arises, if at all, when individuals make agreements with each other. Such an interpretation dismisses, for one reason or another, Hobbes's claim that the laws of nature are God's commands. It might be said, for instance, that Hobbes asserts this to appease religious readers, but that it is not essential to his philosophical argument. The most extreme secular interpretation is that Hobbes is a closet atheist who intentionally tries to subvert the belief in God and the practice of religion. Whatever the case may be, the secular interpretation finds a way to make God irrelevant to Hobbes's primary philosophical positions.

The Religious Interpretation

Religious interpreters of Hobbes's philosophy claim not only that God plays a central role in his philosophical arguments, but also that his faith in Christian beliefs was genuine. So, for example, some religious interpreters assert that God is the lynchpin in Hobbes's theory of moral obligation. The laws of nature, accordingly, are morally obligatory because they are commandments of God. Some religious interpreters claim that one of Hobbes's main goals was to prevent the use of distorted Christian faith for seditious political ends. Consequently, Hobbes spent a great deal of time rationally defending his interpretation of Scripture and showing how it supported his political arguments. Rather than being an aside, religious issues were at the heart of Hobbes's project. To ignore the role of God and religious concepts in

Hobbes's philosophy, it is argued, would result in a seriously inadequate and incomplete interpretation. Theological issues, it is argued, permeate Hobbes's political thinking. In *Leviathan*, for example, the last two books are exclusively devoted to theological issues. More importantly, however, the religious interpreters claim that theological premises are important to Hobbes's main philosophical arguments. So the moral force of Hobbes's laws of nature would be non-existent unless God has a natural command over humans. Through creative interpretation, one may excise Hobbes's religious premises and still present a viable 'Hobbesian' argument; nevertheless, such an argument would be one that Hobbes *might have* presented *if* he were trying to present arguments free of theological presuppositions. This, according to the religious interpreters, was not the case.

Passages to Consider
Comments and Questions on Passages 1 and 2

Some secular interpreters have argued that Hobbes was an atheist who was trying to subvert belief in God. Given the dangerous consequences of professing atheism in the seventeenth century, it was necessary for Hobbes to communicate his message secretly. Hobbes would reveal the pieces of a puzzle, so to speak, and then allow the reader to draw the proper conclusion. Passages 1 and 2 provide two puzzle pieces that connect together to show that there is no such thing as true religion. True religion, according to Passage 1, represents a religion whose imagined beliefs about God correspond to the way God really is. Yet, in Passage 2, Hobbes claims that it is not possible to imagine God at all. If we cannot have an image of God and if true religion requires a correct image of God, then it seems to follow that there cannot be a true religion. Do you believe that Hobbes was secretly trying to communicate this message? How might a religious interpreter of Hobbes resolve the apparent inconsistency of Hobbes's statements?

Passage 1
Fear of power invisible, feigned by the mind, or imagined from tales publicly allowed, [is] religion; not allowed, [it is] superstition. And when the power imagined is truly such as we imagine, [it is] true religion (*L* 6.124).

Passage 2

For as a man that is born blind, hearing men talk of warming themselves by the fire, and being brought to warm himself by the flame, may easily conceive and assure himself, there is something there which men call fire and is the cause of the heat he feels, but [he] cannot imagine what it is like, nor have an idea of it in his mind, such as they that have seen it. So also by the visible things in this world, and their admirable order, a man may conceive there is a cause of them which men call God and yet not have an idea, or image, of him in his mind (*L* 11.167).

Comments and Questions on Passages 3 and 4

It has been suggested that Hobbes was trying to subvert belief in all religions, including Christianity. One may find evidence for this view in Hobbes's comments on miracles, prophecy and divine revelation. According to Hobbes, the ability to perform miracles is not a sufficient sign of a true prophet. In addition, there seems to be no certain way to determine whether someone is a prophet or not. Divine revelation, in other words, is highly suspect. According to his explicit claims, Hobbes is attacking the foundation of other religions apart from Christianity. Yet, does he not also cast doubt on Christian beliefs as well? In Passage 3, Hobbes points out that religion requires a foundational belief in a holy person, but if the signs or 'tokens' of divinity are called into question, then the religion itself may be called into question. In Passage 4, Hobbes concludes that there are no real signs to determine whether someone is divinely inspired. Despite this claim, he seems to acknowledge that Jesus was a true saviour and that the writers of the Holy Scriptures were inspired. Does Hobbes have reasons to believe that Christianity is rationally superior to other religions? What philosophical reasons, if any, does Hobbes give that would allow one to accept that Jesus was a true prophet of God?

Passage 3

For seeing all formed religion, is founded at first, upon the faith which a multitude has in some one person whom they believe not only to be a wise man and to labor to procure their happiness, but also to be a holy man, to whom God himself vouchsafes to declare his will supernaturally; It follows necessarily, when they that have the government of religion shall come to have either the wisdom of those men, their sincerity, or their love suspected; or they shall be unable to show any probable token of divine revelation that the Religion which they desire to uphold must be suspected likewise and (without the fear of the civil sword) contradicted and rejected (*L* 12.179).

Passage 4
Seeing therefore miracles now cease, we have no sign left, whereby to acknowledge the pretended revelations or inspirations of any private man; nor obligation to give ear to any doctrine, farther than is conformable to the Holy Scriptures, which since the time of our savior, supply the place and sufficiently recompense the want of all other prophecy (*L* 32.414).

Comments and Questions for Passages 5 and 6

An important philosophical issue for interpreters of Hobbes is whether God is necessary for the existence of moral obligation. Secular interpreters claim that a theory of moral obligation can be found in Hobbes's philosophy that does not rely upon God. According to this view, humans *create* moral obligations, or put themselves under moral obligations, when they voluntarily abandon their rights. If I voluntarily give up my right to farm a specific field, then I oblige myself not to do this. In Passage 5, Hobbes offers support for this view. On the other hand, Hobbes claims in Passage 6 that humans frequently oblige themselves through 'words', yet these words have no strength unless they are backed up by force. Religious interpreters claim that God provides the force that makes moral obligation stick. Does the combination of Passages 5 and 6 provide more support for the secular or religious interpretation? Is God necessary for a notion of moral obligation in Hobbes?

Passage 5
And when a man has in either manner abandoned, or granted away his right, then he is said to be obliged, or bound not to hinder those, to whom such right is granted or abandoned, from the benefit of it; and that he *ought*, and it is his duty, not to make void that voluntary act of his own; and that such hindrance is *injustice* and *injury*, as being *sine jure* [without right], the right being before renounced, or transferred (*L* 14. 191).

Passage 6
And these signs [that a person has abandoned a right] are either words only, or actions only, or (as it happens most often) both words and

actions. And the same are *bonds* by which men are bound and obliged – bonds, that have their strength, not from their own nature (for nothing is more easily broken than a man's word) but from fear of some evil consequence upon the rupture (*L* 14.191–2).

III. ENQUIRY: WHY DOES GOD ALLOW EVIL TO EXIST?

The problem of evil presents a complex challenge to those who believe in an omnipotent, benevolent and omniscient God. Our world seems to be filled with a plethora of apparently unexplainable 'evils'. An earthquake strikes a small town and leaves many people dead, injured or homeless; innocent individuals are kidnapped, raped and tortured; children are born with diseases that give them no chance of a healthy or long life. If you believe in a good God who knows everything and is all-powerful, you may have wondered why He (or She) would allow such events to occur. If you have wondered, then you have already confronted the problem of evil. In this section, we will consider three of the traditional solutions to the problem of evil. Whether any of them genuinely solves the problem of evil is for you to decide.

The Free Will Solution

One solution to the problem of evil is to say that evil results from our own free will. God, being benevolent, gave us the faculty of free will as a gift to make our lives inherently more valuable. Without free will, we would theoretically be no more than machines operating in the world according to a strict and predictable pattern. Such a life, it is argued, is vastly inferior to a life with the freedom to decide one's own actions. In other words, it is better to have the freedom to choose between good and evil, even if it has negative results, than not to have this freedom at all. God should therefore not be blamed for the manner in which we use our freedom. Instead, we are completely responsible for evil in the world. While this position has a certain amount of plausibility, one might raise the following questions as a response: Assuming free will is responsible for evil, how does this explain the suffering caused by factors beyond human control? For example, does free will explain why God would allow an earthquake to destroy a village? Why would God allow a baby to become infected with a genetic disease that leads to her slow death?

Is the baby's free will responsible? Or is it the free will of the parents? Further, if God knew before the creation what we would do with our freedom and decided to create us anyway, isn't God really to blame for the resulting evil?

The 'Good Requires Evil' Solutions

Some philosophers have tried to solve the problem of evil by linking together good and evil. So, for example, it has been suggested that humans would be unable to appreciate or understand the good unless evil existed. In a world where each and every human genuinely loved all others, one might argue, no one would be able to grasp the goodness of this love. Similarly, one might argue that the existence of good requires the existence of evil. It is impossible for there to be an 'up' without a 'down', a 'top' without a 'bottom', or 'pain' without 'pleasure'. Likewise, there can be no 'good' without 'evil'. Thus, God's decision to create goodness necessarily included a decision to create evil. In response to the first solution, one could claim that humans could still recognize or appreciate the good if the world consisted of contrasting levels of goods. For example, imagine a world where everyone gets along peacefully, but it is still necessary to do such things as tie one's shoes. In such a world, one could recognize and appreciate the goodness of love by comparing it with tying one's shoes, which is either a very low good or simply a non-good. As a response to the second solution, one needs only to say that the existence of good requires the existence of something that is not good. To say that something is not good, however, is not the same as saying it is evil. Do these responses stand up to further scrutiny?

The 'Evil Leads to Good' Solution

Perhaps God allows evil to exist because it ultimately has a good purpose. Bad things frequently happen and individuals are challenged to overcome them. For example, a town is hit with a devastating earthquake that destroys many homes and businesses. Initially, people are emotionally distraught. Over time, however, the townspeople unite together to rebuild their community and, ultimately, it thrives more than ever. What immediately appeared as a misfortune, in other words, is ultimately revealed as a blessing.

The basic idea is that God presents evil as a challenge for us to over-come which, in the end, makes the evil into a good. In response, however, one could use this mode of reasoning to justify vicious actions. The basic principle at work is that the 'ends justify the means'. If, in other words, the end result turns out to be a good one, then it makes the initial act morally acceptable. Most people would agree that this principle is not necessarily a good one. Assume that a woman is impregnated as a result of rape. Assume further that she decides to carry the baby to term and then gives birth to a healthy son, with whom she has a loving relationship. Does this mean that the rapist's actions should be considered good? If the ends do not justify the means for the rapist, why would they do so for God?

CONCLUSION

In this chapter, the summary of Hobbes's philosophy of religion revealed the following points: (1) natural reason reveals that God is the first cause of the universe; (2) although we can know that God exists, we cannot know any of His qualities; (3) the authority to interpret God's word must be granted to the sovereign to avoid civil conflict; (4) superstition is religion that is not allowed; and (5) God creates morality through His will. After the summary, two inter-pretations of Hobbes's philosophy of religion were presented. Although some interpreters believe religion is inconsequential to Hobbes's philosophy, others believe his views of God are at the heart of it. The chapter concluded with an enquiry into the problem of evil.

CHAPTER 7

CONCLUSION

In this book, you have been introduced not only to the main ideas of Hobbes's philosophy, but also to the philosophical activities of interpretation and enquiry. One of my goals in writing this book has been to assist you in developing your own interpretation of Hobbes. As we have seen, many of Hobbes's ideas are subject to a variety of interpretations, each with its own strengths and weaknesses. As you answered the various interpretative questions raised in this book, you may have discovered certain connections among your answers. You may have discovered, in other words, that your interpretation of Hobbes's philosophy on one issue will have affected your interpretation on another issue. For example, if you interpreted Hobbes's laws of nature as moral laws that impose moral obligations, rather than as prudential precepts that simply recommend beneficial actions, then you may have been inclined to interpret them as divine commands. Now that you have a more comprehensive picture of Hobbes's philosophy, I encourage you to re-evaluate your interpretative positions. This is especially important because, for the most part, the interpretative questions in this book were raised in isolation.

Unlike the previous chapters, this chapter includes only a summary and interpretation section. In the first section of this chapter, I summarize some important connections among the interpretative questions raised in this book. The second section raises a final interpretative question: Do the various branches of Hobbes's philosophy constitute a 'unified system'? One cannot address this question without a holistic view of his philosophy; it is therefore an appropriate interpretative question with which to finish. A number of scholars have questioned whether Hobbes's philosophy is supposed to be a 'unified system' whose various branches depend, in some way, on the other branches. Does political philosophy rely upon the discoveries made in natural and moral philosophy? Does moral philosophy rely on presuppositions of natural philosophy? Are the three branches of Hobbes's philosophy independent sciences? Is there a logical unity to Hobbes's philosophy? These questions are part and parcel of what may be called the 'problem of unity', which will be addressed in the second section.

I. SUMMARY: CONNECTIONS AMONG THE INTERPRETATIVE QUESTIONS

The following questions were raised in the Interpretation sections of this book.

- What is Hobbes's theory of truth?
- Is Hobbes a psychological or a tautological egoist?
- Are Hobbes's laws of nature prudential precepts or moral obligations?
- Does Hobbes implicitly accept a limited sovereign?
- Does God play a central role in Hobbes's philosophy?

Let us take a brief look at connections among some of the answers to these questions.

Hobbes's Theory of Truth and his Philosophy

Hobbes, as we have seen, could be interpreted as holding either a correspondence or a conventional theory of truth. According to the correspondence theory, a true statement accurately describes a real feature of the world. If the statement 'all humans are animals' is true, then all humans really are animals. The conventional theory, by contrast, claims that truth is simply a matter of word usage; more specifically, if the subject is 'contained' within the predicate (as Hobbes would say), then the statement is true. In this case, truth expresses a relationship between words. 'All humans are animals' is true, for example, because the meaning of 'human' is included within the meaning of 'animal'. The difference between these two theories is quite dramatic, as we have seen, so deciding which theory Hobbes holds has important implications for interpreting the rest of his philosophy. If Hobbes accepts a conventional theory of truth, then one might question whether any of his philosophical statements describe reality: Are humans really egoistic? Should a sovereign have absolute power? Is the world composed only of material bodies? If Hobbes's answers to such questions are true by definition, one might ask, why should one accept the definitions? If Hobbes is interpreted as holding a conventional view of truth, there is no good answer to this question. Thus, it would be difficult to evaluate any of Hobbes's philosophical ideas if they were not descriptive of reality. In the comments on the other interpretative issues, I will assume that Hobbes holds a correspondence view of truth, at least when it comes to his own philosophical claims.

Hobbes's Egoism and the Political Argument

Hobbes certainly believes that humans are generally selfish by nature. The question, however, is whether Hobbes believes that *all* voluntary actions of *all* humans are *always* motivated by the selfish desire for personal gain. As we have seen, there are two answers to this question. According to the psychological egoist interpretation of Hobbes, every human act is motivated by such a desire. The tautological egoist interpretation, by contrast, says that humans may act on unselfish motives. Your interpretation on this issue could affect your interpretation of Hobbes's political argument. Is it necessary that *all* individuals seek their own personal gain for Hobbes's political argument to work? This question arises because Hobbes's political argument is grounded on universal claims. For example, Hobbes says that the state of nature will become a 'war of *all* against *all*', '*every* man will dread and distrust each other', and 'nature is so arranged that *all* desire good for themselves'.[1] Even though Hobbes speaks of 'all' people and 'every' person, one might claim that his political argument does not require that *all* people are egoistic, but only that *most* people are egoistic. But is this claim right? Would there be a 'war of all against all' if *most* people were egoistic? Would we need an absolute sovereign if only most people were selfish?

Hobbes's Laws of Nature and the Role of God

As we have seen, there are two contrasting interpretations of Hobbes's laws of nature. On the one hand, the laws of nature could be interpreted as prudential precepts that suggest actions that promote an individual's self-interest. Prudential precepts say one ought to do something if one wishes to attain one's own good. On the other hand, the laws of nature could be interpreted as morally obligatory commands. In this case, one ought to do something simply because it is the right thing to do. The question of the moral status of the laws of nature is intertwined with the question of God's role in Hobbes's philosophy. If the laws of nature are morally obligatory commands, one might ask, who is the author of such commands? One may find an easy answer to this question by assuming that God does play an important role in Hobbes's philosophy. Thus, it seems that one's interpretation of Hobbes's laws of nature affects one's interpretation of God's place in Hobbes's philosophy, and vice versa.

II. INTERPRETATION: DO THE BRANCHES OF HOBBES'S PHILOSOPHY CONSTITUTE A UNIFIED SYSTEM?

In *De Cive*, Hobbes claims that he intended to present his philosophy in three separate stages, corresponding to the main branches of his philosophy. 'In the first', he says, 'I would have treated of *body* and its general properties; in the second of *man* and his special faculties and affections; in the third of *civil government* and the duties of subjects' (*Ci* Preface. 102–3). As it turned out, Hobbes published his political philosophy before the other two stages, even though it was supposed to come last chronologically. The reason for its early appearance, Hobbes said, was the brewing conflict in England between king and parliament. With civil war looming, Hobbes hoped that the publication of his political philosophy might help ease the tense situation. In any event, there is an interesting debate in Hobbes scholarship concerning the relationship among the different branches of his philosophy. According to some scholars, who may be called the 'systematic interpreters', Hobbes's intention of presenting the three parts of his philosophy *in a specific order* suggests that the branches have a logical connection with each other. More specifically, it is believed that natural philosophy provides a logical foundation for moral philosophy, which, in turn, provides the logical foundation for political philosophy.[2] Opponents of this interpretation, who may be called the 'non-systematic interpreters', claim that the various branches of Hobbes's philosophy are independent sciences.[3] After considering these two interpretations, you will have to decide for yourself which interpretation is more reasonable.

The Systematic Interpretation

According to the systematic interpretation, Hobbes's philosophy is basically a chain of arguments that begins with natural philosophy and ends in political philosophy. The systematic interpreters ground their view on Hobbes's use of the resolutive-compositive method. The basic idea of this method, as we have seen, is that to understand something, one must intellectually 'resolve' it into its parts and then recompose it. According to the systematic interpreters, Hobbes begins by resolving the political body into its parts (i.e., human bodies), which are then resolved into their parts (i.e., natural bodies). To understand a political body, in other words, one must first understand human bodies, and to understand human bodies, one must first understand natural bodies. By studying the properties of natural bodies we come to philosophical knowledge of human bodies, and this knowledge, in turn, provides knowledge of political bodies. By recomposing the political body from its parts, to put it yet another way, we come to an understanding of it. As one systematic interpreter claims, Hobbes follows the resolutive-compositive method 'by resolving political society into the motions of its parts – individual human beings – and resolving their motions in turn into imagined or hypothetical or simple forces which, compounded, could be shown to explain them'.[4]

There is good evidence for the systematic interpretation since Hobbes often speaks as if the principles of each science are related to each other as links in a deductive chain. In *De Corpore*, for example, Hobbes claims that the principles of political philosophy are found in moral philosophy: 'the principles of politics consist in the knowledge of the motions of the mind' (*Co* 6.74). Moral philosophy, in turn, seems to be dependent upon the conclusions of physics since 'mental motions' have their 'causes in sense and imagination, which are the subject of physical contemplation' (*Co* 6.73). The principles of civil philosophy, in other words, are discovered by an enquiry into mental motions that, in turn, require a physical investigation into the faculties of sense and imagination. Natural philosophy, according to this interpretation, provides the basis for an understanding of human nature that, in turn, provides the foundation for civil philosophy.

The Non-Systematic Interpretation

In contrast to the systematic interpreters, advocates of the 'non-systematic' interpretation claim that the different parts of Hobbes's system are independent sciences that have no logical connection to each another. The main reason for this claim is Hobbes's assertion that the principles of political philosophy may be known through experience and introspection. In the Preface to *De Cive*, Hobbes claims that even though the work was published 'out of order', it can still stand on its own account. 'Therefore it happens', Hobbes says, 'that what was last in order [i.e., his political philosophy] is yet come forth first in time. And the rather, because I saw that, grounded on its own principles sufficiently known by experience, it would not stand in need of the former [i.e., natural philosophy]' (*Ci* Preface. 103). Another reason to believe that Hobbes's political philosophy is not logically connected to his natural philosophy is that the former is supposedly *normative*, while the latter is *descriptive*. As we have seen, a *descriptive* statement is one that *describes* a given thing or state of affairs. In physics, for example, scientists attempt to describe what the world is really like. A *normative* (or *prescriptive*) statement *prescribes* a certain course of action; it informs us of what we ought to do. Philosophers often point out that one cannot derive a prescriptive statement from a descriptive one. To put it another way, it is not possible to derive an 'ought' from an 'is'. For example, just because it *is* the case that men make more money than women, does not mean that it *ought* to be the case. Hobbes's political philosophy, some might argue, is supposed to inform us of what we *ought* to do when it comes to political matters. This kind of statement cannot be derived from physics. Thus, Hobbes's political philosophy is logically independent of his natural philosophy.

Passages to Consider
Comments and Questions for Passage 1

In Passage 1, Hobbes describes the method of his political philosophy. He says that to understand political matters properly, one must 'dissolve' the commonwealth and study human nature. It seems, in other words, that moral philosophy is a stepping-stone to political philosophy. He points out that experience of human nature reveals that humans naturally 'dread and distrust' each other. This 'fact' of human nature, as we have seen, is a foundational principle in Hobbes's political philosophy. Interestingly, Hobbes does not say here that a proper understanding of human nature requires a physical study of natural bodies. He does not say, in other words, that natural philosophy is necessary for moral philosophy. Instead, Hobbes says that the principles of human nature are 'known by experience', suggesting that they are not known by an investigation into natural bodies in general. Thus, according to this passage, it would seem that political philosophy is dependent upon moral philosophy, but not on natural philosophy. At first sight, the fact that the principles of human nature are known by experience seems to discount the systematic interpretation because natural philosophy does not seem to be a necessary part of Hobbes's political and moral philosophy. An advocate of the systematic interpretation, however, might claim that Hobbes is speaking loosely. For example, I could say that I 'know' by 'experience' that dark clouds bring rain. Nevertheless, true knowledge of why this happens depends upon a deeper investigation into the natural world. In other words, I do not really know whether dark clouds bring rain until a scientific investigation proves it. Perhaps Hobbes is using a similar mode of speaking. He may 'know' by 'experience' that humans will dread and distrust each other, but only a deeper investigation into the physical nature of the world will prove it. Does this response seem consistent with Passage 1? Or, does Passage 1 do serious damage to the systematic interpretation?

Passage 1
Concerning my method, I thought it not sufficient to use a plain and evident style in what I have to deliver, except I took my beginning from the very matter of civil government and thence proceeded to its generation and form and the first beginning of justice. For everything is best understood according to its constitutive causes. For as in a watch, or some such small engine, the matter, figure, and motion of the wheels cannot be well known, except it be taken asunder and viewed in parts; so to make a more curious search into the rights of states and duties of subjects, it is necessary, I say, not to take them asunder, but yet that they may be considered as if they were dissolved; that is, that we rightly understand what the quality of human nature is, in what matters it is, in what not, fit to make up a civil government and how much men must be agreed

amongst themselves that intend to grow up in a well-grounded state. Having therefore followed this kind of method, in the first place I set down for a principle, by experience known to all men and denied by none, to wit, that the dispositions of men are naturally such that, except they be restrained through fear of some coercive power, every man will distrust and dread each other; and as by natural right he may, so by necessity he will be forced to make use of the strength he hath, toward the preservation of himself (*Ci* Preface. 98–9).

Comments and Questions for Passage 2

Leo Strauss is a Hobbes scholar who advocates the non-systematic interpretation. He says that Hobbes's political philosophy is independent of natural philosophy 'because its principles are not borrowed from natural science, are not, indeed, borrowed from any science, but are provided by experience, by the experience which every one has of himself, or, to put it more accurately, are discovered by the efforts of self-knowledge and self-examination of every one'.[5] In Passage 2, Hobbes suggests that the way to understand principles of human nature is through self-inspection. Does this passage confirm Strauss's view? Or, could one find a reasonable interpretation of this passage that still allows for the systematic interpretation?

Passage 2
But there is another saying not of late understood, by which they [people] might learn to truly read one another, if they would take the pains; and that is, *nosce teipsum* (read thyself) which was not meant, as it is now used, to countenance either the barbarous state of men in power towards their inferiors or to encourage men of low degree to a saucy behavior towards their betters, but to teach us the similitude of the thoughts and passions of one man to the thoughts and passions of another, [so that] whosoever look into himself and considers what he does, when he does think, opine, reason, hope, fear, etc., and upon what grounds, he shall thereby read and know what are the thoughts and passions of all other men upon like occasions . . . But let one man read another by his actions never so perfectly, it serves him only with his acquaintance, which are but few. He that is to govern a whole nation must read in himself not this or that particular man, but mankind, which, though it be hard to do, harder than to learn any language or science, yet, when I have set down my reading orderly and perspicuously,

the pains left another will only be to consider if he also finds not the same in himself. For this kind of doctrine, admits no other demonstration (*L* Introduction. 82–3).

Comments and Questions on Passage 3

As further evidence for the non-systematic interpretation, one could refer to Hobbes's claim in Passage 3 that the principles of political philosophy are known by experience. In this passage, Hobbes explains why he published *De Cive*, which contains his moral and political philosophy and is supposed to be 'last in order', before the other parts of his philosophy. Although Hobbes say that his political and moral philosophy does not 'stand in need' of natural philosophy, one might still wonder why it was supposed to come last in time. In other words, why would there even be an order to the three branches of philosophy to begin with, if each of them is independent from the others?

Passage 3
Therefore it happens, that what was last in order [i.e., Hobbes's political and moral philosophy], is yet come forth first in time. And the rather, because I saw that, grounded on its own principles sufficiently known by experience, it would not stand in need of the former [i.e., natural philosophy] (*Ci* Preface. 103).

CONCLUSION

Is Hobbes's philosophy a 'unified' system that logically progresses from the study of natural bodies to human bodies to political bodies? To answer this question, you must reconsider the main elements of Hobbes's philosophy. Like every other interpretative question raised in this book, an adequate solution requires you to read Hobbes's texts carefully and to decide for yourself. This question of interpretation, however, requires you to consider Hobbes's philosophy as a whole, to consider his intentions both philosophically and historically, and to determine the specific relationship among the various parts of his philosophy. Hopefully, you now have your own understanding of Hobbes's philosophy, your own way of interpreting his thought, and your own way of enquiring into philosophical issues. Thus, this final problem I leave for you to answer on your own.

NOTES

2. HOBBES'S EPISTEMOLOGY

1 For more on the role of geometry in Hobbes, see: W. Sacksteder, 'Hobbes: The Art of Geometricians', *Journal of the History of Philosophy*, 18 (1980), 131–46.
2 J. Aubrey, *Aubrey's Brief Lives*, O.L. Dick (ed.). Harmondsworth: Penguin, 1972, p. 230.
3 For more on the notion of scientific demonstration in Hobbes, see: D. Hansen, 'The Meaning of "Scientific Demonstration" in Hobbes' Science', *History of Political Thought*, 11 (1990), 587–626.
4 For an example of this interpretation, see: A.P. Martinich, *Thomas Hobbes*. Oxford: Oxford University Press, 1997, pp. 97–8.
5 For an example of this interpretation, see: F.S. McNeilly, *The Anatomy of Leviathan*. London: St Martin's Press, 1968, p. 63; D. Boonin-Vail, *Thomas Hobbes and the Science of Moral Virtue*. Cambridge: Cambridge University Press, 1994, p. 31.
6 R. Descartes, 'Third Set of Objections with the Author's Replies' in *The Philosophical Writings of Descartes*, Cottingham, Stoothoff and Murdoch (trans.). Cambridge: Cambridge University Press, 1984, p. 126.
7 ibid.

3. HOBBES'S METAPHYSICS

1 For more on nominalism in Hobbes, see: G. K. Callaghan, 'Nominalism, Abstraction, and Generality in Hobbes', *History of Philosophy Quarterly* (2001), 18.
2 J. Watkins, *Hobbes's System of Ideas*. London: Hutchinson & Co., 1965, p. 107.
3 For more on the role of mechanism in Hobbes's explanation of human behaviour, see: M. Karskens, 'Hobbes's Mechanistic Theory of Science, and its Role in his Anthropology', in J.G. van der Bend (ed.), *Thomas Hobbes: His View of Man*. Amsterdam: Rodopi B.V., 1982; L.T. Sarasohn, 'Motion and Morality: Pierre Gassendi, Thomas Hobbes,

and the Mechanical World-View', *Journal of the History of Ideas*, 46 (1985), 363–79.

4 For more on the notion of endeavour in Hobbes, see: W. Sacksteder, 'Speaking About Mind: *Endeavour* in Hobbes', *The Philosophical Forum*, 11 (1979), 65–79.

5 T. Hobbes, 'Third Set of Objections with the Author's Replies' in R. Descartes, *The Philosophical Writings of Descartes*, vol. 2. Cottingham, Stoothoff and Murdoch (trans.). Cambridge: Cambridge University Press, 1984, p. 126.

6 For more on this interpretative issue, see: B. Gert, 'Hobbes, Mechanism, and Egoism,' *Philosophical Quarterly*, 15 (1965), 341–9; B. Gert, 'Hobbes and Psychological Egoism', *Journal of the History of Ideas*, 28 (1965), 503–20; T. Lott, 'Motivation and Egoism in Hobbes', *Kinesis*, 6 (1974), 112–25.

7 T. Hobbes, *De Homine* in B. Gert. (ed.), *Thomas Hobbes: Man and Citizen*. Indianapolis: Hackett Publishing, 1991, p. 48.

8 ibid., pp. 48–9.

9 Hobbes, 'Third Set of Objections', p. 126.

10 R. Descartes, *The Philosophical Writings of Descartes*, p. 17.

11 ibid., p. 54.

12 ibid., p. 122.

13 ibid.

14 ibid.

15 ibid.

4. HOBBES'S MORAL PHILOSOPHY

1 For a different reading of Hobbes's moral philosophy than I present here, see: R.E. Ewin, *Virtue and Rights: The Moral Philosophy of Thomas Hobbes*. San Francisco: Westview Press, 1991.

2 T. Hobbes, *De Homine* in B. Gert (ed.), *Thomas Hobbes: Man and Citizen*. Indianapolis: Hackett Publishing, 1991, p. 69.

3 For more on the relationship between Hobbes's natural science and moral philosophy, see: D. Boonin-Vail, *Thomas Hobbes and the Science of Moral Virtue*. Cambridge: Cambridge University Press, 1994; G. Herbert, *Thomas Hobbes: The Unity of Scientific and Moral Wisdom*. Vancouver: University of British Columbia Press, 1989.

4 For an example of this interpretation, see: D. Gauthier, *The Logic of Leviathan: The Moral and Political Theory of Thomas Hobbes*. Oxford: Clarendon Press, 1969.

5 For an example of this interpretation, see: H. Warrender, *The Political Philosophy of Hobbes: His Theory of Obligation*. Oxford: Clarendon Press, 1957.

6 J. Locke, *Second Treatise of Government*. Cambridge: Hackett Publishing, 1980, p. 8.

7 Ibid.

8 Ibid., p. 9.

9 *ST* 2.4.
10 Ibid.
11 Ibid., p. 10.
12 Ibid., p. 12.

5. HOBBES'S POLITICAL PHILOSOPHY

1   For more on the political covenant in Hobbes, see: G. Kavka, *Hobbesian Moral and Political Theory*. Princeton, NJ: Princeton University Press, 1986; J. Hampton, *Hobbes and the Social Contract Tradition*. Cambridge: Cambridge University Press, 1986; S. Kraus, *The Limits of Hobbesian Contractarianism*. Cambridge: Cambridge University Press, 1993.
2   For more on the concept of sovereignty in Hobbes, see: C. Johnson, 'The Hobbesian Conception of Sovereignty and Aristotle's Politics', *Journal of the History of Ideas*, 46 (1985), 327–47.
3   See J. Hampton, *Hobbes and the Social Contract Tradition*, pp. 98–105.
4   For more on this issue, see: A.P. Martinich, *Thomas Hobbes*. New York: St Martin's Press, 1997, pp. 44–9.
5   Ibid., p. 47.

6. HOBBES'S PHILOSOPHY OF RELIGION

1   For a comprehensive look at Hobbes's philosophy of religion, see: A.P. Martinich, *The Two Gods of Leviathan*. Cambridge: Cambridge University Press, 1992.
2   T. Hobbes, *Behemoth* in W. Molesworth (ed.), *The English Works of Thomas Hobbes of Malmesbury*. London: John Bohn, 1846, vol. 6, p. 186.
3   Ibid., p. 252.
4   Ibid., p. 362.
5   Ibid., p. 173.
6   Ibid.
7   Ibid., p. 190.
8   Ibid.
9   For examples of this interpretation, see: D. Gauthier, *The Logic of Leviathan: The Moral and Political Philosophy of Hobbes*. Oxford: Clarendon Press, 1969; J. Watkins, *Hobbes's System of Ideas*. London: Hutchinson and Co., 1965.
10 For examples of this interpretation, see: H. Warrender, *The Political Philosophy of Thomas Hobbes: His Theory of Obligation*. Oxford, Clarendon Press, 1965; A.P. Martinich, *The Two Gods of Leviathan*.

7. CONCLUSION

1   T. Hobbes, *De Homine* in B. Gert (ed.), *Thomas Hobbes: Man and Citizen*. Indianapolis: Hackett Publishing, 1991, p. 48.

2   For examples of the systematic interpretation of Hobbes, see the fol-
    lowing texts: G. Herbert, *Thomas Hobbes: The Unity of Scientific and
    Moral Wisdom*. Vancouver: University of British Columbia Press, 1989;
    M.M. Goldsmith, *Hobbes's Science of Politics*. New York: Columbia
    University Press, 1966; J. Watkins, *Hobbes's System of Ideas*. London:
    Hutchinson and Co., 1965.
3   See, for example, T. Sorell, *Hobbes*. London: Routledge and Kegan Paul,
    1986; G. Shelton, *Morality and Sovereignty in the Philosophy of Hobbes*.
    New York: St Martin's Press, 1992.
4   C.B. Macpherson, 'Introduction to *Leviathan*', in C.B. Macpherson
    (ed.), *Leviathan*. Harmondsworth: Penguin, 1968, p. 27.
5   L. Strauss, *The Political Philosophy of Hobbes: Its Basis and Its Genesis*.
    Chicago: University of Chicago Press, 1963, p. 7.

BIBLIOGRAPHY

Baumgold, Deborah. *Hobbes's Political Theory*. Cambridge: Cambridge University Press, 1988.
—— 'When Hobbes needed History'. *Hobbes and History*. Eds. G. A. J. Rogers and Tom Sorrell. Routledge: London, 2000, 25–43.
Bodin, Jean. *On Sovereignty: Four Chapters from the Six Books of the Commonwealth*. Ed. and trans. Julian H. Franklin. Cambridge: Cambridge University Press, 1992.
Brandon, Eric. 'Hobbes and the Imitation of God'. *Inquiry* 44.2 (2001), 223–226.
Brown, Clifford W. Jr. 'Thucydides, Hobbes, and the Derivation of Anarchy'. *History of Political Thought* 8.1 (1987), 33–62.
Burns, Norman T. *Christian Mortalism from Tyndale to Milton*. Cambridge: Harvard University Press, 1972.
Calvin, John. *Commentaries on the first book of Moses called Genesis*. Grand Rapids: William B. Eerdmans, 1965.
—— *Institutes of the Christian Religion*. Trans. Ford Lewis Battles. Grand Rapids: William B. Eerdmans, 1986.
—— *Psychopannychia*. In *Selected Works of John Calvin*. Ed. Henry Beveridge. Vol. 3. Grand Rapids: Baker Book House, 1983, 413–490.
Chappel, Vere. *Hobbes and Bramhall on Liberty and Necessity*. Cambridge: Cambridge University Press, 1999.
Curley, Edwin. 'Calvin and Hobbes, or, Hobbes as an Orthodox Christian'. *Journal of the History of Philosophy* 34.2 (1996), 257–271.
—— '"I Durst Not Write So Boldly" or How to read Hobbes' theological-political treatise'. *Hobbes e Spinoza*. Ed. Daniela Bostrenghi. Naples: Bibliopolis, 1992, 497–593.
—— 'Reflections on Hobbes: Recent Work on His Moral and Political Philosophy'. *Journal of Philosophical Research* 15 (1989–90), 169–250.
—— 'Reply to Professor Martinich'. *Journal of the History of Philosophy* 34.2 (1996), 285–287.
Connor, Robert W. *Thucydides*. Princeton: Princeton University Press, 1984.
Descartes, René. *The Philosophical Writings of Descartes*. Eds. John Cottingham, Robert Stoothoff and Dugald Murdoch. Vol. 2. Cambridge: Cambridge University Press, 1984.

Franklin, Julian H.. *Jean Bodin and the Rise of Absolutist Theory*. Cambridge: Cambridge University Press, 1973.

Gauthier, David P. *Morals by Agreement*. Oxford: Clarendon Press, 1986.

—— *The Logic of Leviathan*. Oxford: Oxford University Press, 1969.

Geach, Peter. 'The Religion of Thomas Hobbes'. *Religious Studies* 17 (1981), 549–558.

Grant, Robert M. and Tracy, David. *A Short History of the Interpretation of the Bible*. Philadelphia: Fortress Press, 1984.

Hampton, Jean. *Hobbes and the Social Contract Tradition*. Cambridge: Cambridge University Press, 1986.

Harvey, Martin. 'Hobbes's Conception of Natural Law'. *The Southern Journal of Philosophy* 37 (1999), 441–460.

Hobbes, Thomas. *An Answer to a Book Published by Dr Bramhall, Late Bishop of Derby; Called the 'Catching of the Leviathan'*. In *The English Works of Thomas Hobbes*. Ed. William Molesworth. Vol. 4. London: Routledge, 1994.

—— *Behemoth*. Chicago: University of Chicago Press, 1990.

—— *Considerations upon the Reputation, Loyalty, Manners, and Religion, of Thomas Hobbes, of Malmesbury, written by himself, by way of a letter to a learned person*. In *The English Works of Thomas Hobbes*. Ed. William Molesworth. Vol. 4. London: Routledge, 1994.

—— *De Cive*. In *Man and Citizen*. Ed. Bernard Gert. Indianapolis: Hackett Publishing, 1991.

—— *De Corpore*. In *The English Works of Thomas Hobbes*. Ed. William Molesworth. Vol. 1. London: Routledge, 1994.

—— *The Correspondence of Thomas Hobbes*. Ed. Noel Malcolm. 2 vols. Oxford: Oxford University Press, 1994.

—— *Human Nature and De Corpore Politico*. Ed. J. C. A. Gaskin. Oxford: Oxford University Press, 1994.

—— *Leviathan*. Ed. Edwin Curley. Indianapolis: Hackett Publishing, 1994.

—— *The Questions Concerning Liberty, Necessity, and Chance*. In *The English Works of Thomas Hobbes*. Ed. William Molesworth. Vol. 5. London: Routledge, 1994.

Jesseph, Douglas M. *Squaring the Circle*. Chicago: University of Chicago Press, 1999.

Johnston, David. *The Rhetoric of Leviathan*. Princeton: Princeton University Press, 1986.

Kavka, Gregory. *Hobbesian Moral and Political Theory*. Princeton: Princeton University Press, 1986.

—— 'The Reconciliation Project'. *Morality, Reason and Truth*. Eds David Copp and David Zimmerman. Totowa: Rowman and Allanheld, 1984, 297–319.

Klosko, George and Rice, Daryl. 'Thucydides and Hobbes's State of Nature'. *History of Political Thought* 6.3 (1985), 405–409.

Lloyd, S.A. *Ideals as Interests in Hobbes's Leviathan*. Cambridge: Cambridge University Press, 1992.

Lockyer, Roger. *Tudor and Stuart Britain: 1471–1714*. London: Longmans, Green and Co., 1954.

Luther, Martin. *Disputation Against Scholastic Theology*. In *Martin Luther's Basic Theological Writings*. Ed. Timothy F. Lull. Minneapolis: Fortress Press, 1989.

—— *Disputation on the Power and Efficacy of Indulgences*. In *Martin Luther's Basic Theological Writings*. Ed. Timothy F. Lull. Minneapolis: Fortress Press, 1989.

—— *Preface to the Old Testament*. In *Martin Luther's Basic Theological Writings*. Ed. Timothy F. Lull. Minneapolis: Fortress Press, 1989.

MacPherson, C.B. *The Political Theory of Possessive Individualism: Hobbes to Locke*. Oxford: Clarendon Press, 1962.

Martinich, A.P. *Hobbes: A Biography*. Cambridge: Cambridge University Press, 1999.

—— 'On the Proper Interpretation of Hobbes's Philosophy'. *Journal of the History of Philosophy* 34.2 (1996), 273–283.

—— *The Two Gods of Leviathan*. Cambridge: Cambridge University Press, 1992.

Nagel, Thomas. 'Hobbes's Concept of Obligation'. *The Philosophical Review* 68.1 (1959), 68–83.

Overton, Richard. *Mans Mortalitie*. Ed. Harold Fisch. Liverpool: Liverpool University Press, 1968.

Pelikan, Jaroslav. *The Christian Tradition*. Vol. 4. Chicago: University of Chicago Press, 1984.

Pocock, J.G.A. 'Time, History, and Eschatology in the Thought of Thomas Hobbes'. *Politics, Language and Time*. New York: Atheneum, 1973, 148–201.

Rogerson, John, Christopher Rowland, Barnabas Lindars SSF. *The Study and Use of the Bible*. The History of Christian Theology Series. Vol. 2. Grand Rapids: William B. Eerdmans Publishing Co., 1988.

Rupp, E. Gordon, trans. and ed. *Luther and Erasmus: Free Will and Salvation*. Philadelphia: Westminster Press, 1969.

Schneewind, J. B. *The Invention of Autonomy*. Cambridge: Cambridge University Press, 1998.

Skinner, Quentin. *Reason and Rhetoric in the Philosophy of Hobbes*. Cambridge: Cambridge University Press, 1996.

—— *The Foundations of Modern Political Thought*. 2 vols. Cambridge: Cambridge University Press, 1978.

Slomp, Gabriella. 'Hobbes, Thucydides and the Three Greatest Things'. *History of Political Thought* 9.4 (1990), 565–586.

Smith, David L. *A History of the Modern British Isles, 1603–1707*. Oxford: Blackwell, 1998.

Sommerville, Johann P. *Thomas Hobbes: Political Ideas in Historical Context*. New York: St Martin's Press, 1992.

Strauss, Leo. *Persecution and the Art of Writing*. Chicago: University of Chicago Press, 1952.

—— *The Political Philosophy of Hobbes*. Chicago: University of Chicago Press, 1952.

Suarez, Francisco. *De Legibus*. In *Selections from Three Works*. Oxford: Clarendon Press, 1944.

Taylor, A. E. 'The Ethical Doctrine of Hobbes'. *Hobbes Studies*. Ed. K. C. Brown. Cambridge: Harvard University Press, 1965, 35–55.

Trevor-Roper, Hugh. *From Counter-Reformation to Glorious Revolution*. Chicago: University of Chicago Press, 1992.

Tuck, Richard. *Hobbes*. Oxford: Oxford University Press, 1989.

Warrender, Howard. *The Political Philosophy of Hobbes*. Oxford: Clarendon Press, 1957.

Williams, George Huntston. *The Radical Reformation*. Philadelphia: The Westminster Press, 1962.

Williams, Penry. *The Later Tudors: England 1547–1603*. Oxford: Clarendon Press, 1995.

Zarka, Yves Charles. 'First philosophy and the foundation of knowledge'. *The Cambridge Companion to Hobbes*. Ed. Tom Sorell. Cambridge: Cambridge University Press, 1996, 62–85.

INDEX